Foundations
◆
The Bible

Center for Biblical Leadership

White Wing Publishing House

Tennessee • Peru • Mexico • Guatemala
Philippines • Dominican Republic • India

ACD
1997

Foundations–The Bible
Copyright ©1997
Published by White Wing Publishing House and Press
P. O. Box 3000
Cleveland, TN 37320-3000
(423) 559-5425 • 1-800-221-5027
All rights reserved
Cover Illustration: Perry Horner
First Published, 1997

ISBN #1-889505-05-6

Preface

This Foundations Course (Bible Section) by the Center for Biblical Leadership is presented with the hope that it will provide a basic knowledge of the principles to be embraced by those who are committed to Jesus Christ. We acknowledge freely His headship of the Church He is building and we are dedicated to follow Him faithfully.

Being rather broad in scope, there is not an attempt to deal with many of the specifics which subsequently it will be necessary to explore more fully. It will be revised and updated from time to time to assure current relevance to the needs of our people.

We sincerely appreciate all the research and work that has been done in the preparation of this foundations course. It is presented as a foundational tool with the prayer that it will contribute to a more knowledgeable and a more competent leadership for God's people.

This course could be valuable locally for group or individual study. May God's grace add richness to what we are presenting here which will make our thrust into the harvest more effective.

BILLY D. MURRAY
General Overseer

INTRODUCTION

This course of study is designed to serve as a contribution to the ongoing process of Christian education and leadership development in the Church of God of Prophecy. It is available to anyone who desires a systematic program to increase their knowledge of the Bible. This course of study should be of interest to those desiring help in preparing for the ministry, individuals who want to further their understanding of the foundation of the faith, and could also be used by local congregations seeking resources and outlines for Bible study.

The course of study consists of measurable goals and objectives. It should be noted that, since the resources are direct quotes, the outlines and footnotes will appear just as they do in the original. These are not the only places where this individual can find information but are chosen for their suitability as introductory texts. At the end of this booklet a self-administered examination will be found that will demonstrate the individual's knowledge of the subject.

The following is the complete set of goals and objectives that have been established for this course of study:

The Bible

Goal: The Individual will demonstrate an understanding of the nature, history, background, and content of the Bible.

Unit One—The individual will demonstrate an understanding of the **nature** of the Bible by:
a) listing reasons why it is important to study the Bible
b) defining the nature of biblical revelation
c) naming the two main divisions of the Bible
d) listing in order the names of the books of the Bible
e) naming the various literary divisions of the Bible

Unit Two—The individual will demonstrate an understanding of the **history** of the Bible by:

a) naming the original languages of the Bible
b) dentifying language, origin, and author of the following translations of the Bible: Septuagint, Vulgate, Authorized Version
c) naming the traditional Hebrew divisions of the Scriptures
d) explaining the significance of the Old Testament for the Christian, stating its relation to and difference from the New Testament
e) describing the process of canonization
f) entifying the significance of the following persons connected with the history of the English Bible: John Wycliffe, William Tyndale, King James I

Unit Three—The individual will demonstrate an understanding of the **background** of the Bible by:
a) summarizing the differences between the people of Israel and the early Christians
b) describing the significance of the Egyptians, Canaanites, Assyrians, Babylonians, and Persians for understanding the Bible
c) identifying characteristics of the Pharisees and Sadducees
d) locating the following geographical regions on a map of the world: Egypt, Palestine, Assyria, Babylonia, Persia, Asia Minor
e) locating on a map, and indicating the importance of, the cities of Jerusalem, Nazareth, Capernaum, Bethlehem; the provinces of Galilee, Samaria, Judea, Decapolis, and Perea; and the Sea of Galilee and the Dead Sea
f) identifying the significance of the following people from the Intertestamental period: Alexander the Great, Ptolemy, Antiochus Epiphanies, Mattathias, Judas Maccabeus, Pompey, and Herod the Great
g) identifying traditional authors of the books of the Bible

Unit Four—The individual will demonstrate an understanding of the **content** of the Old Testament by:
a) identifying the theme, and, where appropriate, the key events and people of each book of the Old Testament

b) constructing a chronological outline of the main events in the history of the people of Israel
c) describing the life and significance of the following people: Abraham, Isaac, Jacob, Joseph, Moses, Joshua, Samuel, Saul, David, Solomon, Isaiah, Jeremiah, Ezekiel, Nehemiah, and Daniel
d) describing the significance of the following events: The Call of Abraham, The Exodus from Egypt, The Establishment of the Covenant at Sinai, The Institution of the Levitical Sacrifices, The Conquest of Canaan, The Rule by Judges, The Establishment of the Monarchy, The Division of the Kingdom, The Exile in Babylon, The Return from Captivity
e) naming the Ten Commandments

Unit Five—The individual will demonstrate an understanding of the **content** of the New Testament by:
a) identifying the theme, and, where appropriate, the key events and people of each book of the New Testament
b) describing the life and significance of the following people: John the Baptist, Jesus, Paul, Peter, John the Apostle, James (the brother of Jesus)
c) describing the significance of the following events: The Birth of Christ, The Crucifixion and Resurrection, The Day of Pentecost, The Correspondence of Apostle Paul
d) constructing a chronological outline of the main vents in the life of Christ
e) locating on a map the missionary journeys of the apostle Paul
f) naming the Beatitudes

It is the purpose of this course of study that the individual will find it useful in the development of their understanding of God's truth and purposes. In the final analysis it is one's application of this knowledge through prayer and a vital relationship with Christ that makes it valuable. Proverbs 2:1-7 says, "My son, if thou wilt receive my words, and hide my commandments with thee; So that thou incline thine ear unto wisdom, and apply thine heart to understanding; Yea, if thou criest after knowledge, and liftest up thy voice for understanding; If thou seekest her as silver, and searchest for her as for hid treaures; Then shalt thou understand the fear of the LORD, and find the knowledge of God. For the LORD giveth wisdom: out of his mouth cometh knowledge and understanding. He layeth up sound wisdom for the rightcous: he ia a buckler to them that walk uprightly."

CONTENTS

INSTRUCTIONS

This course of study is designed to be used by an individual who wants to further his or her understanding of the foundations of the faith, one who is in the process of obtaining ministerial credentials, or a local church who wants to use it as a study course. The examination, found in the back of the book, has been developed to demonstrate one's knowledge of the objective. They have been written to be self-administered, open-book examinations, and should be completed using the Resource Guide included in the course, or other appropriate materials. If the registration form, which is included in the back of the book, is used, one (1) Leadership Development Unit (LDU) may be earned for the completion of this course.

Individual Study *(NOT a minister, ministerial candidate, or candidate for Certified Teacher)*

This course of study may be taken as an individual study by anyone who desires to improve their understanding of the Bible. In this case, the individual will be responsible to read the assigned materials and take the examination at his or her own pace. There will be no Certificate of Completion awarded for an individual study.

Individual Study *(Ministers, ministerial candidates, or candidates for Certified Teacher)*

A minister, ministerial candidate, or candidate for the Certified Teacher Certificate may earn one (1) Leadership Development Unit for the completion of this course. To earn this credit, the individual will need to register for this course of study with the state/regional/national office (registration form is included with examination in the back of the book). Once the course of study has been completed, the examination should be reviewed by the person's pastor and submitted to the state/regional/national office. A Certificate of Completion will be granted by the state/regional/national office and appropriate records kept. The overseer and Ministerial Review Board may exempt an applicant from this course if significant knowledge can be validated through other equivalent educational programs.

Group Courses

Persons who take this course in an approved group study will receive a Certificate of Completion to validate the completion of the requirements. Such group studies will be conducted by the Pastor or an instructor approved by the Pastor. The instructor will be responsible for teaching the course, giving and grading exams, and sending the completed Examination Report Form to the Center for Biblical Leadership at the International Offices. The instructor will find the answer keys and Examination Report Form in the instructor's packet which was provided at purchase for those taking a group study.

In order for those participating in a study course to be granted a Certificate of Completion, the following requirements must be met:

1) The instructor must be the Pastor or approved by the Pastor.
2) The course must consist of at least ten hours of instruction, and the student must not have more than two hours of valid absences.
3) The student must read the text and successfully complete the examinations which accompany the text.

The Bible

GOAL: THE INDIVIDUAL WILL DEMONSTRATE AN UNDER-STANDING OF THE NATURE, HISTORY, BACKGROUND, AND CONTENT OF THE BIBLE.

Central to the role of leadership and calling into the ministry is the recognition that the minister must be an individual of the Word of God. In instructions given by the apostle Paul to Timothy, he said, "But continue thou in the things which thou hast learned and hast been assured of, knowing of whom thou hast learned them; And that from a child thou hast known the holy scriptures, which are able to make thee wise unto salvation through faith which is in Christ Jesus. All scripture is given by inspiration of God, and is profitable for doctrine, for reproof, for correction, for instruction in right-eousness: That the man of God may be perfect, throughly furnished unto all good works" (2 Tim. 3:14-17). This admonition was quickly followed by the charge to "Preach the word; be instant in season, out of season; reprove, rebuke, exhort with all longsuffering and doctrine" (2 Tim. 4:2). These admonitions reveal that the Bible is the heart of ministry. The importance of such instructions is as significant today as when they were given. Anyone who seeks to be involved in the ministry must have a knowledge of the Bible in order to be effective.

This course of study is designed to provide the individual with a foundational knowledge of the Word of God. It will introduce the individual to the nature, history, background, and content of the Bible. Each of these aspects of the Bible will be looked at in a separate unit of study. At the beginning of the units of study a list of specific objectives will be given to guide the learning process in an effort to achieve this goal.

Following the objectives will be a selection of readings from which these objectives may be achieved. The selected reading will serve as a resource from which one may pursue the objectives. Individuals may also have at their disposal other such material that they may wish to study. They should utilize whatever material is appropriate to achieve the objectives.

The last section of this course is a self-administered examination that will be used to ensure that you are able to meet the stated objectives. This exam will serve to reinforce the learning of significant items. The individual should look at this exam with the thought of learning the expected knowledges.

As this course is being completed, great care should be taken to seek God in prayer so that more than simply intellectual understanding of the material is received. The same Spirit who inspired the authors in writing the Bible will be with the individual who is open to His leading. It is hoped that this may be a means of realizing the prayer of Ephesians 1:17-19:

That the God of our Lord Jesus Christ, the Father of glory, may give unto you the spirit of wisdom and revelation in the knowledge of him [Christ]: The eyes of your understanding being enlightened; that ye may know what is the hope of his calling, and what the riches of the glory of his inheritance in the saints, And what is the exceeding greatness of his power to us-ward who believe, according to the working of his mighty power.

The Nature of the Bible

Unit One

Objectives:

The individual will demonstrate an understanding of the *nature* of the Bible by:

- listing reasons why it is important to study the Bible.
- defining the nature of biblical revelation.
- naming the two main divisions of the Bible.
- listing, in order, the names of the books of the Bible.
- naming the various literary divisions of the Bible.

Resource Guide for Learning Goals and Objectives

UNIT ONE: THE NATURE OF THE BIBLE

Objective: The individual will demonstrate an understanding of the nature of the Bible by listing reasons why it is important to study the Bible.

Raymond M. Pruitt, Fundamentals of the Faith, *pp. 45, 46, 48*

Though there is a growing interest in studying the Scriptures, there are still some people who have the notion that systematic Bible study is for ministers, teachers, and missionaries. Nothing could be further from the truth. The Bible is God's personal message to every Christian believer (1 Thess. 2:13).

From Fundamentals of the Faith, Raymond M. Pruitt (White Wing Publishing House, 1981). Used by permission.

It is the Book through which God communicates to us. John Wesley summed up his own personal commitment to the Bible as the one central Book of his life in the following statement from his *Journal:*

I am a creature of a day, passing through life, as an arrow through through the air. I am a spirit come from God, and returning to God; just hovering over the great gulf till a few moments hence, I am no more seen! I drop into an unchangeable eternity!

I want to know one thing, the way to heaven: how to land safe on that happy shore. God Himself has condescended to teach the way: for this very end Jesus came from heaven. He hath written it down in a book! Oh, give me that book! At any price, give me the Book of God! I have it. Here is knowledge enough for me. Let me be *homo unius libri* (a man of one book).

Here then I am far from the busy ways of men. I sit down alone: only God is here. In His presence I open, I read this Book, for this end, to find the way to heaven. Is there a doubt concerning the meaning of what I read? Does anything appear dark or intricate? I lift up my heart to the Father of Lights. Lord, is it not Thy Word? 'If any lack wisdom, let him ask of God; that giveth liberally and upbraideth not.' 'If any will to do his will, he shall know,' I am willing to do; let me know Thy will.

I then search after, and consider parallel passages of scripture, 'comparing spiritual things with spiritual.' I meditate thereon, with all the attention and earnestness of which my mind is capable. If any doubt still remains, I consult those who are experienced in the things of God, and then the writings whereby, being dead, they yet speak, and what I thus learn, that I teach.[1]

It is the key to abundant life on earth, and eternal joy in the world to come. Someone has written:

This Book contains the mind of God; the state of man; the way of salvation; the doom of sinners; and the happiness of believers. Its doctrines are holy; its precepts are binding; its stories are true; and its decisions are immutable. Read it to be wise; believe it to be safe; and practice it to be holy. It contains light to direct you; food to support you; and comfort to cheer you. It's the traveller's map, the pilgrim's staff; the pilot's compass; the soldier's sword; and the Christian's charter. Here is paradise restored; heaven opened; and the gates of hell disclosed. CHRIST is its grand object; our good its design; and the glory of God its end. It should fill the memory, rule the heart, and guide the feet. Read it slowly, frequently, prayerfully. It is a mine of wealth, a paradise of glory, a river of pleasure. It is given you in life, will be opened at the judgment, and remembered forever. It involves the highest responsibility, will reward the laborer, and condemns all who trifle with its contents![2]

It discovers sin and convicts us of it. The Sandow Institute near London has helped to bring thousands of Britishers back to robust health through its four fundamental steps:

a. diagnosis of the trouble
b. removal of whatever is causing the trouble
c. a carefully prescribed diet
d. a consistent exercise program

This is exactly what the Word of God does for us, beginning with a diagnosis of our condition (Heb. 4:12; 2 Tim. 3:16; James 1:23, 24).

It shows us how to be cleansed from the pollution of sin, which is the cause of our trouble (1 John 1:9; Ps. 119:9; John 15:3; 17:17; Eph. 5:25, 26).

It nourishes our inner self with spiritual nourishment. Thus, it provides the diet necessary to spiritual health. A graphic example of how the living and the written Word redeems and sustains us is given in Exodus 12, where the Lord commanded the Passover lamb to be slain and that the blood be struck on "the two side posts and on the upper doorpost of the houses" (v. 7). The blood of the slain lamb saved the Israelites from death and gave them life. But there was more. The flesh of the lamb was to be eaten after it had been roasted with fire. Thus, the strength needed for the pilgrimage of redeemed Israel was provided by **partaking** of the lamb that was slain. The lamb in this context speaks of the incarnate Word of God and the written Word of God (John 1:1; Deut. 8:3; Job 23:12; Jer. 15:16; Acts 20:32; 2 Tim. 4:1-4).

It instructs us in what we ought to do in our spiritual exercise program (Matt. 7:24-27).

It provides us with a sword for victory in the struggle against sin and the devil (Eph. 6:17; Ps. 119:11).

It fosters victorious and fruitful Christian living (Ps. 1:1-3; Josh. 1:8, 9).

It helps us to be powerful in prayer (John 15:7; 2 Tim. 3:14-17).

Objective: The individual will demonstrate an understanding of the nature of the Bible by defining the nature of biblical revelation.

Raymond M. Pruitt, Fundamentals of the Faith, *pp. 23-25*

The doctrine of the inspiration of Scripture gives the Christian faith a place to stand which is more secure than human reason, the scientific method, or any court of law. We believe as we do, not because we always understand our beliefs, but because we believe the Bible is the Word of God, and that it is entirely and verbally God-given in the original autographs, without error or fault in **all** of its statements.

Man being what he is, fallen and corrupted by sin, and God being what He is, holy, loving, and merciful, we would expect a revelation from God to man which would embody the essential truth by way of an absolutely reliable and infallible source. Man's estrangement from God leaves him ignorant of God's purposes and means of salvation apart from the Scriptures, without which he is incapable of knowing whether he can be saved, and if so, how.

Since it is so absolutely vital to our eternal destiny to know how to find acceptance with God and to know His will for us, the doctrine of the inspiration of the Scriptures is fundamental to whether or not the Bible speaks with absolute and unquestioned authority.

From Fundamentals of the Faith, *Raymond M. Pruitt (White Wing Publishing House, 1981). Used by permission.*

I. The Definition of Inspiration

1. **What is inspiration?** This term is based upon the Greek word *theopneustos*, found only in 2 Timothy 3:16, where it is translated, "given by inspiration of God." This means that the written Word of God is just as authoritative and as infallible as the oral pronouncements of God Himself.

a. We must distinguish between revelation and inspiration. **Revelation** is the imparting of truth, by God to man, which could not be otherwise known (cf. 1 Cor. 2:10). **Inspiration** refers to the reception and recording of truth (2 Pet. 1:20, 21).

It is possible to have revelation without inspiration, such as when the apostle John heard the voices of the seven thunders, but was forbidden to write what they said (Rev. 10:3, 4).

It is also possible to have inspiration without revelation, as when writers of both the Old and New Testaments sometimes wrote down what they had witnessed with their own eyes, or had discovered by research (1 John 1:1-4; Luke 1:1-4). Originality is not a necessary qualification for Scriptures; inspiration is.

Through revelation God communicated His Word to "holy men of God." Through inspiration they "spake as they were moved by the Holy Ghost" (2 Pet. 1:21). Being filled with the actuating energy of the Holy Spirit, they wrote the revelation precisely as God had given it, without error.

Admittedly, there is mystery in how the Word was actually transmitted from the mind of God through the inspired writer to the written page. One of the soundest explanations is that inspiration is "that inexplicable power which the divine Spirit put forth of old on the authors of Holy Scripture, in order to their guidance even in the employment of the words they used, and to preserve them alike from all error and from all omission."[3] The Prime Mover in inspiration is God. "For the prophecy came not in old time by the will of man: but holy men of God spake as they were moved by the Holy Ghost (2 Pet. 1:21). God **moved** (revelation) and man **spake** (inspiration); God **revealed** (revelation) and man **recorded** (inspiration). Inspiration involved man in the sense of his response to the move of the Spirit, whereas revelation is solely the activity of God. Inspiration includes the activity of God, the response of the writer, and the product of the written Word.

b. The difference between inspiration and authority should also be noted. Sometimes what is inspired is not to be taken as a standard for belief and conduct. For example, the words of Satan to Eve (Gen. 3:4, 5), and to Christ (Matt. 16:22), were recorded by inspiration, but they are not truth to live by; they are only a true account of what was said. Such statements do not reflect the mind of God. The same would be true of any passage which is taken out of context and given an interpretation which differs from the one it had in its original setting.

c. Inspiration also differs from illumination. Illumination has to do with the apprehension and understanding of truth (1 Cor. 2:13, 14; Ps. 119:18). In revelation God unveils His truth; in inspiration it is received and recorded; in illumination truth is understood.

d. Illumination usually accompanies inspiration, but sometimes it does not (see 1 Pet. 1:11, 12).

Objective: The individual will demonstrate an understanding of the nature of the Bible by naming the two main divisions of the Bible.

Raymond M. Pruitt, Fundamentals of the Faith, *p. 16*

The Two Divisions of the Bible

The terms Old Testament and New Testament are titles for the old and new covenants (*berith,* Heb.; *diatheke,* Gk.). "Covenant" is a designation of the Mosaic law, "the book of the covenant" (2 Kings 23:2; also 2 Cor. 3:14). The New Testament is "new" because at the death of Jesus the curtain of partition between the holy place and holy of holies in the temple was rent, thus ending the legalism of the law, and grace became the essence of God's relationship with men through Christ, hence "New" Testament (Heb. 12:24).

From Fundamentals of the Faith, Raymond M. Pruitt (White Wing Publishing House, 1981). Used by permission.

The relationship between the two covenants is aptly summarized by St. Augustine: ". . . the Old Testament is revealed in the New, the New is veiled in the Old. . . ." W. Graham Scroggie has noted: "The New is in the Old contained, the Old is in the New explained."

The books of the Bible (39 in the Old Testament, 27 in the New Testament) were written over a period of about 1,600 years by about 36 different writers. This long range of time, diversity of writers, and difference in political, economic, and geographic conditions, makes the unity of the Bible even more amazing.

Objective: The individual will demonstrate an understanding of the nature of the Bible by listing, in order, the names of the books of the Bible.

Holy Bible, Table of Contents

The Books of the Old Testament

Book	Chapters	Book	Chapters
Genesis	50	Ecclesiastes	12
Exodus	40	The Song of Solomon	8
Leviticus	27	Isaiah	66
Numbers	36	Jeremiah	52
Deuteronomy	34	Lamentations	5
Joshua	24	Ezekiel	48
Judges	21	Daniel	12
Ruth	4	Hosea	14
1 Samuel	31	Joel	3
2 Samuel	24	Amos	9
1 Kings	22	Obadiah	1
2 Kings	25	Jonah	4
1 Chronicles	29	Micah	7
2 Chronicles	36	Nahum	3
Ezra	10	Habakkuk	3
Nehemiah	13	Zephaniah	3
Esther	10	Haggai	2
Job	42	Zechariah	14
Psalms	150	Malachi	4
Proverbs	31		

From Fundamentals of the Faith, Raymond M. Pruitt (White Wing Publishing House, 1981). Used by permission.

The Books of the New Testament

Book	Chapters	Book	Chapters
Matthew	28	1 Timothy	6
Mark	16	2 Timothy	4
Luke	24	Titus	3
John	21	Philemon	1
The Acts	28	To the Hebrews	13
Romans	16	The Epistle of James	5
1 Corinthians	16	1 Peter	5
2 Corinthians	13	2 Peter	3
Galatians	6	1 John	5
Ephesians	6	2 John	1
Philippians	4	3 John	1
Colossians	4	Jude	1
1 Thessalonians	5	Revelation	22
2 Thessalonians	3		

Objective: The individual will demonstrate an understanding of the nature of the Bible by naming the various literary divisions of the Bible.

Raymond Pruitt, Fundamentals of the Faith, *pp. 17-19*

The Old Testament's 39 books are divided into the following sections (the books are listed in order with a theme title and a key verse or passage):

The Books of the Law (*Pentateuch,* Gk., "five-volumed book")

Genesis—The Book of Beginnings (1:1)
Exodus—God's Deliverance of, and Covenant With, Israel (3:8; 12:23-31; 19:4-6)
Leviticus—The Manual of the Priesthood (19:2)
Numbers—Wilderness Wandering (14:26-30)
Deuteronomy—A Rehearsal of the Law (11:26-28)

The Historical Books (12 books)

Joshua—The Conquest of Canaan (1:2, 3, 6)
Judges—The First 300 Years in the Land of Promise (2:14-19)

From Fundamentals of the Faith, *Raymond M. Pruitt (White Wing Publishing House, 1981). Used by permission.*

Ruth—Beginning of the Family of David from Which Came Our Kinsman-Redeemer, the Lord Jesus Christ (1:15, 16; 4:10, 22)
1 Samuel—The Beginning of the Kingdom (8:19-22)
2 Samuel—The Reign of David (7:8-16)
1 Kings—Solomon's Reign and the Beginning of the Kingdom (2:12; 11:13)
2 Kings—The History of the Divided Kingdom (17:7, 8, 18-23)
1 Chronicles—Priestly Perspective of David's Reign (11:9)
2 Chronicles—Priestly History of the Southern Kingdom (1:1; 36:15-21)
Ezra—The Return From Captivity (1:1, 2)
Nehemiah—The Rebuilding of Jerusalem (4:6)
Esther—The Origin of the Feast of Purim ('lots') (9:20-32)

The Poetic Books (5 books)

Job—The Problem of Suffering (1:21-22)
Psalms—The Hymnbook of God's People (7:17)
Proverbs—The Book of Wisdom (1:7)
Ecclesiastes—Worthy Objectives for Living (1:1-3; 12:13, 14)
Song of Solomon—The Beauty of Wedded Love (7:6)

The Major Prophets (5 books)

Isaiah—The Statesman Prophet of the Messianic Age (61:1-3)
Jeremiah—The Prophet of Judah's Declining Years (1:4-10)
Lamentations—Jeremiah's Dirge Over Jerusalem's Desolation (1:1)
Ezekiel—The Prophet of the Captivity (15:7, 8)
Daniel—The Prophet of World Empires (7:1)

The Minor Prophets (12 books) (These are called "minor," not because they are of lesser importance, but because the books are shorter.)

Hosea—The Unfaithfulness of Israel (3:1; 2:13-16)
Joel—Prophecies Concerning the Day of the Lord (2:28-32)
Amos—The Inevitable Judgment of God Against Sin (4:11, 12)
Obadiah—The Doom of Edom (v. 4)
Jonah—A Mission of Mercy to Nineveh (3:2)
Micah—The Prophet of Universal Peace (5:2; 7:18-20)
Nahum—The Doom of the Assyrian Kingdom (3:18, 19)
Habakkuk—The Doom of the Chaldean Kingdom (2:14)
Zephaniah—The Prophet of Judgment and Desolation (1:14-16)

Haggai—The Prophet of the Restoration Temple (2:4)
Zechariah—The Prophet of the Messianic Kingdom (9:9; 14:3, 4)
Malachi—God's Love for a Backsliding People (1:1-5)

The New Testament's 27 books are divided into the following sections:

Biographical (4 books)

Matthew—The Gospel of Christ the King, Son of David (1:1)
Mark—The Gospel of Christ the Servant of the Lord (10:45)
Luke—The Gospel of Christ the Son of Man (19:10)
John—The Gospel of Christ the Son of God (20:31)

History (1 book)

Acts—The History of the Early Church (1:8)

Pauline Epistles (13 books)

Romans—The Gospel of Christ (1:16, 17)
1 Corinthians—The Standard for Christian Conduct (15:58)
2 Corinthians—The Vindication and Conduct of the Ministry (5:20)
Galatians—The Law and the Gospel of Grace (1:6-9)
Ephesians—The Unity of the Church (4:4-6)
Philippians—The Joy of Knowing Christ (1:21)
Colossians—The Preeminence of Christ (1:15-19)
1 Thessalonians—The Model Church (1:7-10)
2 Thessalonians—The Second Coming of Christ (2:2)
1 Timothy—The Standard for Church Order (3:14-16)
2 Timothy—Paul, A Good Soldier of Jesus Christ (4:6-8)
Titus—The Order of God's House (1:5)
Philemon—Christian Brotherhood Exemplified (vv. 15-18)

General Epistles (8 books)

Hebrews—The Superiority of the Son of God (7:24-26)
James—Practical Christian Faith (2:18)
1 Peter—Victory Over Suffering (1:6-9)
2 Peter—Christian Growth (3:17, 18)
1 John—The Father's Love Letter to His Children (4:7-10)

2 John—Walking in Truth and Love (v. 6)
3 John—Christian Hospitality Toward Those Who Walk in Truth (5-8)
Jude—Contending for the Faith (v. 3)

Prophetical (1 book)

Revelation—The Return of Christ and the Establishment of His Kingdom (1:18, 19)

The History of the Bible

Unit Two

Objectives:

The individual will demonstrate an understanding of the **history** of the Bible by:

- naming the original languages of the Bible.
- identifying language, origin, and author of the following translations of the Bible: Septuagint, Vulgate, Authorized Version.
- naming the traditional Hebrew divisions of the Scriptures.
- explaining why it is the basis of authority for the believers.
- describing the process of canonization.
- identifying the significance of the following persons connected with the history of the English Bible: John Wycliffe, William Tyndale, King James I.

Resource Guide for Learning Goals and Objectives

Unit Two: The History of the Bible

Objective: The individual will demonstrate an understanding of the history of the Bible by naming the original languages of the Bible.

Raymond M. Pruitt, Fundamentals of the Faith, p. 41

Old Testament written in Hebrew. God gave the Old Testament Scriptures in Hebrew, except for brief passages in

---

From Fundamentals of the Faith, Raymond M. Pruitt (White Wing Publishing House, 1981). Used by permission.

Ezra 4:8; 6:18; 7:12-26, and Daniel 2:4; 7:28, which are in Aramaic, the language of diplomacy during the time of Persian supremacy. A verse in Jeremiah 10:11 was written in the Chaldean tongue during the Babylonian threat.

The Hebrew language was "the language [literally, the lip] of Canaan" (Isa. 19:18), and was ideally suited as the medium for transporting God's message to the people. Of the genius of that tongue, Bruce notes:

> Biblical Hebrew does not deal with abstractions but with facts of experience. It is the right sort of language for the record of the self-revelation of God who does not make Himself known by philosophical propositions but by controlling and intervening in the course of human history. Hebrew is not afraid to use daring anthropomorphisms when speaking of God. If God imparts to men the knowledge of Himself, He chooses to do so most effectively in terms of human life and human language.
> . . . Indirect speech is unknown to Biblical Hebrew; all speech is reported in the direct form. . . .[4]

4. **New Testament written in Greek.** The New Testament Scriptures were written in Greek, which was the language of the Roman empire. Thus, it was ideally suited for the evangelistic outreach of the church. Through the medium of the Greek language the gospel of Christ was disseminated throughout the Roman world into the farthest outposts of civilization.

***

Objective: The individual will demonstrate an understanding of the history of the Bible by identifying language, origin, and author of the following translations of the Bible: Septuagint, Vulgate, Authorized Version.

Bible Training Institute, General Bible Study, p. 11

Translations of the Bible. One of the earliest translations is known as the *Septuagint.* This is a *Greek* translation of the Old Testament, completed in Alexandria about 285 B.C. It is called the Septuagint from a popular belief that the work of translation was done by seventy Greek-speaking Jewish scholars.

***

Bible Training Institute, *General Bible Study.*

In 400 A.D. Jerome completed, in Bethlehem, a Latin translation of the entire Bible, this translation becoming known as the **Vulgate**. This was the standard translation in the Roman Catholic Church for over a thousand years. During the Middle Ages, the Bible was locked up in the Latin language, unavailable to the common people. The Catholic Church frowned on any attempt to translate the Scripture into a common language for Latin was considered the only language sacred and holy enough to express the words of God.

However, toward the close of the Dark Ages there arose a great demand for translations intelligible to the common people. One of the earliest English translations is that of John Wycliffe and his followers (known as the Lollards), completed sometime after his death in 1384. Martin Luther was making his German translation at about the same time as William Tyndale was completing his English version around A.D. 1530.

But the monumental work in common language translation was the Authorized Version of A. D. 1611, commonly known as the **King James Version**. This version is the work of forty-seven scholars appointed by King James I of England and it has continued to hold first place in popularity throughout the English-speaking world for over three hundred years. It is a masterpiece of fidelity to the original Greek and Hebrew texts and is considered a literary work without equal or parallel in the English language.

Objective: The individual will demonstrate an understanding of the history of the Bible by naming the traditional Hebrew divisions of the Scriptures.

Hector Ortiz, The Living Word, pp. 4, 5

The ancient Hebrew form of the Old Testament was arranged differently than the present English Old Testament of thirty-nine books. The Hebrew and English Old Testaments contain all of the same thirty-nine books; only the grouping or arrangement is different. In the early development of the Hebrew Bible, there was a twofold division: *The Law* and *The*

Hector Ortiz, *The Living Word* (Cleveland, TN: White Wing, 1984). Used by permission.

Prophets (Matt. 5:17; Luke 16:16). However, in the process of time, a threefold classification of the Hebrew Scriptures was developed (Luke 24:44). The Hebrew divisions, it seems, were flexible and not rigid. The threefold classification numbered twenty-four books; or twenty-two books if Ruth is attached to Judges, and if Lamentations is attached to Jeremiah. Regardless of the classifications of these books, they were reverenced as God's words. The following chart shows the arrangement of the threefold classification of the present Hebrew Bible according to the Masoretic text with its Hebrew names.

THE HEBREW OLD TESTAMENT ARRANGEMENT

The Law (Torah)	The Prophets (Nebhiim)	The Writings (Kethubhim)
1. Genesis	A. Former Prophets	A. Poetical Books
2. Exodus	1. Joshua	1. Psalms
3. Leviticus	2. Judges	2. Proverbs
4. Numbers	3. Samuel	3. Job
5. Deuteronomy	4. Kings	B. Five Rolls (Megilloth)
	B. Latter Prophets	1. Song of Songs
	1. Isaiah	2. Ruth
	2. Jeremiah	3. Lamentations
	3. Ezekiel	4. Esther
	4. The Twelve	5. Ecclesiastes
		C. Historical Books
		1. Daniel
		2. Ezra-Nehemiah
		3. Chronicles

(Note: This is the arrangement in modern Jewish editions of the Old Testament. Cf. The Holy Scriptures, According to the **Masoretic Text***; and Rudolf Kittel and Paul E. Kahle (eds.), Biblia Hebraica).*[5]

The arrangement of the Hebrew Bible is divided according to the rank and official position of the writer, in contrast to how the modern Bible is arranged.

Hector Ortiz, *The Living Word* (Cleveland, TN: White Wing, 1984). Used by permission.

The transition from the ancient Hebrew Bible arrangement (Old Testament) to the present one was the result of the Hebrew Scriptures being translated into Greek at Alexandria, Egypt (280-150 B.C.). This famous translation, known as the Septuagint, signified by LXX, introduced the fourfold classification according to subject matter (The Law, History, Poetry, Prophets). Since the Septuagint was widely used in ancient times, the same format of a fourfold classification system was used in arranging the order of the New Testament. The final step in standardizing the fourfold classification of the Bible came when Jerome translated the Bible into Latin, known as the Vulgate (A.D. 388-405), which was the prevailing Bible translation for at least a thousand years.[6]

Objective: The individual will demonstrate an understanding of the history of the Bible by explaining why it is the basis of authority for the believer.

Perry Gillum and Rob Allen, Issues: A Biblical Perspective: *pp. 10-13*

By an overwhelming majority, most of the people who attend our churches believe in the inerrancy of the Bible—that it was given by the Holy Ghost to holy men of God who wrote under His inspiration—and they therefore, believe that the Bible is our sure guide for living in favor with God. However, not all who believe this are able to show why they believe it. In this section, we will consider some of the evidences for the authority of the Bible.

The Bible itself claims to be the inerrant record of the revelation of God given to holy men who wrote as the Holy Ghost moved them. One text in which the Bible makes this claim is 2 Timothy 3:16: "All scripture is given by inspiration of God, and is profitable for doctrine, for reproof, for correction, for instruction in righteousness." The original language implies that the Scriptures are the direct result of the breathing out of God. In a number of passages the Scriptures are spoken of as the expression of God Himself (Matt. 19:4, 5; Heb. 3:7; Acts 4:24, 25; 13:34, 35; Gal. 3:8; Rom. 9:17).

From *Issues: A Biblical Perspective*, Perry Gillum and Rob Allen (Cleveland, TN: White Wing, 1986). Used by permission.

In several passages the New Testament is clearly given the same authority as the Old Testament. For example, Paul writes in 1 Thessalonians 2:13, "For this cause also thank we God without ceasing, because, when ye received the word of God which ye heard of us, ye received it not as the word of men, but, as it is in truth, the word of God, which effectually worketh also in you that believe." In 2 Peter 3:15,16, that apostle placed Paul's writings in the same category as the Old Testament books: "And account that the longsuffering of our Lord is salvation; even as our beloved brother Paul also according to the wisdom given unto him hath written unto you; As also in all his epistles, speaking in them of these things; in which are some things hard to be understood, which they that are unlearned and unstable wrest, as they do also the other scriptures, unto their own destruction."

In 2 Peter 1:21, Peter writes, "For the prophecy came not in old time by the will of man: but holy men of God spake as they were moved by the Holy Ghost." The word translated "were moved" means the writers of the Holy Scriptures were carried along by the Holy Ghost. The same word is used in Acts 2:2 where Luke describes the coming of the Holy Ghost at Pentecost as a mighty wind. In Acts 27:15,17, he uses the word again to describe the ship that was caught by the storm and was "driven." It did not cease to be a ship, but it was under the control of the wind.

When the Bible speaks of itself, it clearly indicates that it is not man's words about God, but God's words about man and to man. To hear the Bible is to hear God speaking. This is the conclusion we get from reading the Bible regarding its message. The men of the Bible regarded the Word of God as absolute and infallible. To obey the Bible is to obey God. To disobey is to stand against God.

Jesus affirmed the inerrancy and authority of the Bible. When He was tempted by Satan in the wilderness, He quoted from Deuteronomy three times (Matt. 4:1-11). On a number of other occasions He appealed to the Scriptures to defend His actions—when He cleansed the Temple (Mark 11:15-17), and when He explained His submission to the cross (Matt. 26:53, 54), for example. Jesus claimed absolute authority for His own teaching: "It was said. . .but I say unto you" (5:21, 22). "For he taught them as one having authority, and not as the scribes" (7:29). "Heaven and earth shall pass away: but my words shall not pass away" (Mark 13:31).

He saw His life as a fulfillment of Scripture and consciously submitted to what was written. When He began His public ministry, He quoted from Isaiah 61:1, 2, "The Spirit of the Lord is upon me, because he hath anointed me to preach the gospel to the poor; he hath sent me to heal the brokenhearted, to preach deliverance to the captives, and recovering of sight to the blind, to set at liberty them that are bruised, To preach the acceptable year of the Lord" (Luke 4:18,19). He emphasized that this prophecy was fulfilled in His ministry. After His resurrection, He chided the apostles because of their slowness to understand and to believe the Scriptures: "O fools, and slow of heart to believe all that the prophets have spoken: Ought not Christ to have suffered these things, and to enter into his glory? And beginning at Moses and all the prophets, he expounded unto them in all the scriptures the things concerning himself" (24:25-27).

In these and many other passages, Jesus clearly regarded the Old Testament as being absolutely infallible in every detail, and submitted Himself to everything which was spoken concerning Him.

Additional evidence for the authority of the Bible.[7] John Wesley said that the Bible must have been written by either bad men or devils, or good men or angels, or by God. He showed that it could not have been written by bad men or demons, for it condemns them to hell for all eternity, nor could it have been written by good men or angels, for they would not say, "Thus saith the Lord," when it was they who said it; it must, therefore, have been written by God.

The character of God and the need of man would indicate that God would provide a trustworthy guide for man to find the way back to God and to the fullness of life which God desires for him.

The dynamic life-changing influence of the Bible is one of the strongest evidences of its divine origin. Thousands upon thousands have been converted, and whole societies have been changed by the teaching and preaching of God's Word.

The unsurpassed unity and harmony of the Bible is proof of its divine origin. A book with such divine perfection despite the great diversity of its backgrounds and training of its writers can best be explained as being the product of a supernatural mind; namely, God. No other book but the Bible can claim such unity from such diverse sources.

Objective: The individual will demonstrate an understanding of the history of the Bible by describing the process of canonization.

Raymond M. Pruitt, Fundamentals of the Faith, *pp. 31-35*

The Canon of The Scriptures

We have considered the doctrine of the inspiration of the Scriptures, how the divine revelation was put in writing, inerrant and infallible in every word, and in its entirety. Now we will focus on how certain writings became a part of the canon of Scripture, and why other writings did not.

Definition

The meaning of the canon. *Inspiration* refers to how the books of the Bible received their authority; *canonization* refers to how they received acceptance by the Church. Canonization, then, concerns the recognition and collection of God-breathed authoritative writings into the body of Holy Scripture.

Literally, the word "canon" is derived from the Greek word *kanon*, which is evidently from the Hebrew word *kaneh* "reed." The Greek word *kanon* means a "reed," from which we get "a rod," or "bar." The literal concept provided the basis for the later use of the term to be used metaphorically as "a standard." In grammar, it meant a standard for what grammar ought to be in structure and procedure. In literature, it determined which particular works could be accurately attributed to a specific author. For example, "the canon of Plato" denotes all of the writings which can be definitely attributed to Plato.

The importance of the canon. It should be obvious that literary canons are a safeguard against attributing spurious works to a writer which could distort his position on important subjects. Only his genuine writings reflect his thought. Any person who wanted to successfully propagate a theory in the name of a well-known and accepted writer only needed to get his treatise passed off as a genuine product of the more authoritative author.

From *Fundamentals of the Faith,* Raymond M. Pruitt (White Wing Publishing House, 1981). Used by permission.

Athanasius (c. 293-373 A.D.), a bishop during the 4th century tumult over the question of who Jesus Christ was, is credited with first using the term "canon" in connection with the New Testament books soon after A.D. 350; these he called "the fountains of salvation."[8]

If the Canon of the Bible cannot be established without question, then the authority of its books as "the fountains of salvation" would be unreliable, and we would have no sure and certain authority for our faith, and no dependable guide for standards of conduct. We would be hopelessly lost without the infallible, inerrant Word from God. But because the question of canonicity has been so irrefutably settled, we can confidently, and without apology, declare that "we accept the Bible as the Word of God—believe and practice its teachings rightly divided—the New Testament as (our) rule of faith and practice, government and discipline."

In summary, by the canonicity of a book, we mean its right to a place in the collection of sacred writings which are considered by Christians to comprise the very Word of God (2 Tim. 3:16, 17).

The Test of Canonicity

The development of the canon. During the first three centuries the local churches were generally more or less isolated from each other, and usually they were small. Since there was no printing press, all manuscripts had to be hand-copied, and this meant that the reproduction of copies was a slow and tedious process. The means of communication were slow, but gradually there came into circulation certain manuscripts which were accepted for reading in the churches. A writing which was known to be by one of the apostles, or by someone who was known to and approved by the apostles, was given ready acceptance. Over a period of time, some of these writings, but not all of them, were added to the canon.

It was not until the middle of the fourth century that all the books of the New Testament were universally accepted by all of the churches and their leaders. Those writings which were circulated fell into four groups: (1) *Homologoumena*, books accepted by virtually all as being canonical; (2) *Antilegomena*, books whose authenticity were questioned by some; (3) *Pseudepigrapha*, books which were rejected by practically everyone as being without reliable authority; (4) *Apocrypha*, books which were rated as canonical by some, but were questioned by others. Eusebius made a similar classification, rating some as (1) acknowledged books; some as (2) disputed books; some as (3) spurious books; and others as (4) heretical books, which were "absurd and impious."[9]

The establishment of canonicity. The establishment of the canonicity of a book depends on how its inspiration can be demonstrated. In other words, the fundamental test of canonicity is inspiration. It is "God-breathed" (2 Tim. 3:16), and how can that be known to the complete satisfaction of all concerned?

Determination and recognition. We must distinguish between the *determination* and the *recognition* of canonicity. Canonicity is *determined* by God. The authority of God was given to each of the individual books as the writer recorded what he received through inspiration (2 Pet. 1:21). On this, George Salmon comments:

> It is remarkable fact that we have no early interference of church authority in the making of a Canon; no council discussed this subject; no formal decisions were made. The canon seems to have shaped itself . . . Let us remember that this non-interference of authority is a valuable topic of evidence to the genuineness of our Gospels; for it thus appears that it was owing to no adventitious authority, but *by their own weight*, they crushed all rivals out of existence.[10]

There was no dependence of God upon men to sort out and classify the books that would comprise the canon of Scripture. There was no command of God that this should be done, and no formal agreement by any council or committee of men. Gradually and naturally, the church gathered into a sacred whole all of the writings which it held sacred separately.

Canonicity is recognized, not determined, by men. The basic premise is that a book is valuable because it is canonical; it is not canonical because it is valuable. It was made canonical by God's authority, not man's, and thus it is valuable. As stated previously, a book is canonical because it is inspired.[11]

When the Word of God was written it became Scripture, and, inasmuch as it had been spoken by God, possessed absolute authority. Since it was the Word of God, it was canonical. This which determines the canonicity of a book, therefore, is the fact that the book is inspired of God.

The difference illustrated. The difference between God's determination and man's recognition of the canon of the Scriptures is illustrated by a chart from Geisler and Nix:[12]

The Incorrect View

The Church Is the Determiner of Canon
The Church Is Mother of Canon
The Church Is Magistrate of Canon
The Church Is Regulator of Canon
The Church Is Judge of Canon
The Church Is Master of Canon

The Correct View

The Church Is Discoverer of Canon
The Church Is Child of Canon
The Church Is Minister of Canon
The Church Is Recognizer of Canon
The Church Is Witness of Canon
The Church Is Servant of Canon

Criteria for recognizing canonicity. Men recognized the writings which God had given as Scripture because those writings possessed the characteristics, or marks, of inspiration. That is, they must possess: authority, a living spiritual character, universality, and authenticity.

Authority was established when it was known that the writing was the work of a man of God, either a prophet, an apostle, or one known to and approved by an apostle, and that the writer wrote under divine inspiration.

A book **possessed** a living **spiritual** character, due to its having been "God-breathed" (2 Tim. 3:16), which in turn caused it to have a positive moral and spiritual effect upon its readers. The apocryphal books lacked in this and other characteristics.

The **universality** of a book was demonstrated when its contents were fully applicable to, and accepted by, the people of God everywhere.

Authenticity had to do with both the source and the content of the book. It must be inspired, and if the author is revealed, it must be his work and not the work of an imposter, or by an author who uses a pseudonym. Its contents must be infallibly true.

Objective: The individual will demonstrate an understanding of the history of the Bible by identifying the significance of the following persons connected with the history of the English Bible: John Wycliffe, William Tyndale, King James I.

Hector Ortiz, The Living Word, pp. 107, 109

There was no complete English Bible before the fourteenth century. Prior to John Wycliffe, only portions of certain Scriptures were translated into English.[13] It took the convictions of the Morning Star of the Reformation (John Wycliffe) to accomplish the first English translation of the Bible.

John Wycliffe (A. D. 1330-84)

This doctor of theology is recognized for his deep convictions against the papal claims, and for casting aside his "dry scholastic Latin" in order to reach the English people in their common language. Due to his reformed preaching and teaching, he was relieved of his teaching duties at Oxford.

Wycliffe's outreach to the English people was through the Lollards, who were itinerant preachers (poor priests) that went throughout England preaching the Bible in English. The efforts of this movement produced the Wycliffe translations of the New Testament in A.D. 1380, and the Old Testament in A.D. 1388. The latter translation was completed by Nicholas of Hereford, since Wycliffe died in A.D. 1384. A revision of the first Wycliffe Bible was accomplished by John Purvey, who had served as Wycliffe's secretary, about A.D. 1395. Although these first English Bible translations were made prior to the invention of the printing press, the impact of this work was so great that years after Wycliffe's death, his body was exhumed and burned. His ashes were scattered on the River Swift in A.D. 1428.

Hector Ortiz, *The Living Word* (Cleveland, TN: White Wing, 1984). Used by permission.

William Tyndale (A. D. 1492-1536)

Tyndale's contribution to the transmission of the sacred text is that he was the first to produce a portion of a printed version from the original Hebrew and Greek into English. His persistent courage and dedication is noted in his reply to another's claim that Englishmen would be "better without God's law than without the pope's," to which Tyndale replied, "I defy the pope and all his laws; if God spares my life, ere many years I will cause, a boy that driveth the plough shall know more of the Scripture than thou dost." Because of difficulties, Tyndale could not finish his translation in England. He had to escape to different parts[14] of Europe to complete his project. His English New Testament was printed in Cologne in February A.D. 1526, and had to be smuggled into England. In subsequent years he translated different portions of the Old Testament at great danger to his life. He was kidnapped, imprisoned, found guilty of heresy in August, A.D. 1536, and executed on October 6, while crying out at the stake: "Lord, open the King of England's eyes!" Tyndale's version of the New Testament provided a further base for the subsequent versions, of which the Authorized Version (KJV) is one.

Miles Coverdale (A. D. 1488-1569), Thomas Matthew (A. D. 1500-1555)

Both Coverdale and Matthew, whose real name was John Rogers, were assistants to Tyndale, who published a complete English New Testament. The honor of the first complete, printed, English Bible was the Coverdale edition. The Coverdale edition was not based on the original languages, and the Matthew Bible was a combination of Tyndale's and Coverdale's work, with notes attached. Richard Taverner (A.D. 1505-1575) made a revision of the Matthew Bible, but this work has had little effect on subsequent Bible translations.

The Great Bible (A. D. 1539), The Geneva Bible (A. D. 1557, 1560)

The Great Bible was mainly based on the Coverdale Bible of A.D. 1535. This work was accomplished under the direction of Miles Coverdale, with the approval of Thomas Cranmer and Thomas Cromwell. It became the authorized Bible to be used in the churches of England in A.D. 1538, and the official text for the Anglican's Book of Common Prayers and administration of the sacraments. The second edition of this Bible (seven editions in all) contains a preface by Cranmer, causing it to be known also as Cranmer's Bible.

The Great Bible was superseded by the Geneva Bible, which was produced during the violent and oppressive reign of Mary Tudor. The oppressive condition in England drove many Protestants into exile in Geneva, where John Knox was leading a group in preparing an English version to meet their needs. The New Testament of this work was completed in A.D. 1557; the entire Bible, in A.D. 1560. This Bible had 140 editions, published before A.D. 1644, and it was in the Geneva Bible that *italicized* words were first used. It was the first English Bible to divide chapters into verses. The Geneva Bible became the Bible of the Puritans, and it was denoted as an effort by a committee, as explained in the following: "The distinguishing method of the Geneva Committee had been a system of careful and methodical collaboration, as contrasted with the isolated labours of the pioneers of translation."

While the Geneva Bible became the home Bible in England, the Anglican church, to offset the Puritan efforts, produced a revision of the Great Bible, known as the Bishops' Bible (A.D. 1568). It was given the name of Bishops' Bible due to the fact that most of the translators were bishops. The Bishops' Bible was the Bible used in the churches of England from A.D. 1568 to 1611, and was the official basis for the Authorized Version (KJV).

The King James Version (A. D. 1611)

The state of affairs in England was such that when James VI of Scotland became James I of England, he called the Hampton Court Conference in January, A.D. 1604, to consider the Millenary Petition of the Puritans. This petition was named *millenary* because it contained a thousand signatures setting forth the grievances of the Puritans. It was in this conference that the proposal by John Reynolds (the Puritan president of Corpus Christi College, Oxford) was made, suggesting that a new authorized version of the English Bible be produced for use in the churches, as well as the homes. The endorsement of such a proposal created a selected *committee* of fifty-four revisers, to work in six different companies. (Note: Fifty-four men served on the committee; forty-seven scholars did the actual translations.)

The translators' instructions were to use the Bishops' Bible as their official basis, as well as Tyndale's, Matthew's, Coverdale's, and the Geneva Bible, in the process of translation. The purpose of the translation is described in the following: "Truly (good Christian Reader) we never thought from the beginning, that we should need to make a new translation, nor yet to make a bad one a good one . . . but to make a good one better, or out of many good ones, one principal good one, not justly to be excepted against; that hath been our endeavour, that our mark . . . ." The King James Version (KJV), although technically not a version and not really authorized, became intrinsically the version of the English-speaking Protestants. The KJV was actually revised by the edition of the English Revised Version of 1881-85, which was the basis for the 1901 American StandardVersion (ASV). The ASV was followed by the Revised Standard Version (RSV; New Testament, 1946; Old Testament, 1952), which was a revision based on a "critical text."

The production of new versions and translations, it seems, is an ongoing process, as more manuscripts and evidence from antiquity are discovered. However, great care must be exercised in dealing with the multiplicity of versions and revisions, since the question of interpretation of new evidence is always a critical step in documentation. Multiplied millions have been blessed through the different versions and revisions of God's Word. Nevertheless, in the search for God's perfect will, all will have to depend on the illumination of God's Spirit, to see that "the light of the glorious gospel of Christ, who is the image of God, should shine unto them" (2 Cor. 4:4).

Objectives:

The individual will demonstrate an understanding of the *background* of the Bible by:

- describing the significance of the Egyptians, Canaanites, Assyrians, Babylonians, and Persians, for understanding the Bible.
- identifying characteristics of the Pharisees and Sadducees.
- locating the following geographical regions on a map of the world: Egypt, Palestine, Assyria, Babylonia, Persia, and Asia Minor.
- locating major cities, provinces, and bodies of water on a map of Palestine.
- identifying the significance of the following people from the Intertestamental Period: Alexander the Great, Ptolemy, Antiochus Epiphanes, Mattathias, Judas Maccabeus, Pompey, and Herod the Great.
- identifying traditional authors of the books of the Bible.

Resource Guide for Learning Goals and Objectives

UNIT THREE: THE BACKGROUND OF THE BIBLE

Objective: The individual will demonstrate an understanding of the background of the Bible by describing the significance of the Egyptians, Canaanites, Assyrians, Babylonians, Persians, for understanding the Bible.

David and Pat Alexander, ed., Eerdman's Handbook to the Bible, *pp. 660, 661*

Egyptians

The inhabitants of Egypt had a highly developed civilization matching that of Mesopotamia. When Abraham had contact with Egypt in the Middle Kingdom Period (c. 2100-1800 B.C.) its civilization was already over a thousand years old. It was probably during the Second Intermediate Period (c. 1800-1600 B.C.) that Joseph and his people settled there. The Exodus took place under the New Kingdom (c. 1600-1100 B.C.), probably in the time of the nineteenty dynasty Pharaoh Rameses II (c. 1290-1224 B.C.). Israel is mentioned as one of the nations in Palestine on the so-called "Israel Stele" of his successor Merneptah (c. 1224-1220 B.C.).

By the first millennium B.C., the great days of Egyptian civilization were over. A fresh attempt at Asiatic conquest was made in the tenth century by Sheshonq I (biblical Shishak, 1 Kings 11:29-40; 14:25-26), and Solomon traded with Egypt in the same century (see Cilicians). He also married a Pharaoh's daughter. But though Egyptian rulers intervened in Palestine and Syria after this (2 Kings 19:9; 23:29; 24:1-7; Jer. 37:5-19; 46:1-26; Ezek. 17:11-21), Egypt was now a 'broken reed' (2 Kings 18:21; Isa. 36:6). The country became successively part of the Persian, Hellenistic, and Roman Empires.

Canaanites

These were sedentary inhabitants of Palestine and southern Syria, who had a flourishing urban civilization in the second millennium B.C. The corrupt religion of Canaan, criticized in the Old Testament, is illustrated in texts from Ugarit (modern Ras Shamra). Hebrew is a dialect to the Canaanite language (Isa. 19:18) and the related Ugaritic language greatly helps our understanding of it.

Assyrians

The homeland of these neighbors of the Babylonians was north Mesopotamia. During the second millennium, Assyria came under the rule of Amorites, and c. 1350-1100 B.C. built up a powerful state, exercising some control as far west as the Mediterranean Sea. Its capital was then Ashur, but in

---

883 B.C. Ashurnasirpal II (883-859 B.C.) moved his capital to Calah, modern Nimrod. His successors, including Shalmaneser III (858-824 B.C.), Adad-nirari III (810-783 B.C.), Tiglath-pileser III (or Pul; 744-727 B.C.), Shalmaneser V (726-722 B.C.), all of whom had contacts with Israel, continued there until Sargon II (721-705 B.C.) founded a new capital at Dur-Sharruken (modern Khorsabad). His son Sennacherib (704-681 B.C.) moved the capital to Nineveh. There it remained under Esarhaddon (680-669 B.C.), Ashurbanipal (668-627 B.C., probably the Asnapper of Ezra 4:10), and other minor kings until its destruction in 612 B.C. by the Chaldeans and Medes.

Babylonians

These were the heirs of the Sumerians and Akkadians in southern Mesopotamia. Their capital city was Babylon. The best-known king of the first Babylonian dynasty (of Amorite stock, eighteenth century B.C., roughly the time of Abraham) was Hammurabi, the author of a famous code of laws.

During the early part of the first millennium B.C., the Babylonians were subject to the Assyrians, but c. 612-539 B.C. the Neo-Babylonian, or Chaldean, dynasty dominated Western Asia. Nebuchadnezzar (604-562 B.C.), Amel-Marduk (biblical Evil-Merodach, 561-560 B.C.), Nergal-shar-usar (biblical Nergal-Sharezer, Greek Neriglissar, 559-556 B.C.), and Belshazzar were rulers of this dynasty mentioned in the Old Testament. Babylon fell to Cyrus the Persian in 539 B.C.

Persians

The Persians were an Indo-European-speaking people who conquered the Babylonians in the sixth century B.C. and went on to control an empire stretching from India to the Aegean and Egypt. Their main capital cities were Pasargadae and Persepolis in the mountains of southwest Persia, and the ancient Elamite capital Susa (biblical Shushan, Dan. 8:2; Neh. 1:1; Esther) in the lowland plain. Their liberally administered empire lasted until it became part of the still more extensive empire of Alexander the Great in the fourth century B.C.

Objective: The individual will demonstrate an understanding of the background of the Bible by identifying characteristics of the Pharisees and Sadducees.

Pharisee

People of all nations usually have some type of religion, and people of every era have catered to this approach in an effort to contact the Power that is higher than man to assuage guilt of conscience. Since our concern here is biblical, we shall so pursue, for the impact of the writings of both the Old and New Testaments have left a profound impression upon the peoples of the world. It is impossible to refer to all religions that existed during the short span of the life of Christ on this earth, but it seems appropriate to refer to some of them.

The sect of the Pharisees (if we should call it that) was a Jewish religious, and somewhat political, party that actually emerged in the early second century B.C., and showed prominence during the Maccabean revolt—165-160 B.C., or thereabouts. Their origin may be traced perhaps to an earlier Jewish sect known as the Assideans, or Hassideans—the Greek form of the Hebrew word *Hasidim*— which arose during the third or fourth century B.C., and which sect showed impressively during the Maccabean revolt as recorded in 1 Maccabees 2:42.

At first the Pharisees, it seems, were a protest group against the Hellenistic influence that was invading the ranks of the religious and orthodox Jews who considered themselves successors to Ezra. They believed in a resurrection, but so multiplied trivial precepts and frivolous observances with traditions that the worshiper actually did not know or understand the written law of God, being burdened and clouded with many trifling instructions.

They are referred to as the "separated ones" or Formalists of the Jewish people, numbering six to seven thousand in the time of Christ. They held to temple worship as a national nucleus of religion, but were somewhat pragmatic in the promotion of synagogue worship and observances. They represented the prevailing religious beliefs, views, opinions, and social attitudes of the majority of the Jewish people—in one way or another—holding tenaciously to the oral law and traditions that sometimes

---

From C. T. Davidson, *Upon This Rock*, Vol. I, (Cleveland, TN: White Wing, 1973-76) pp. 128-131. Used by permission.

shamed them and plagued them in spite of their embracing the written law, though seemingly secondary at times, in an effort to protect Judaism.

The Pharisees were a self-righteous sect that liked the attention and praises of men, and did much to polish the outward appearance. They looked with contempt upon other nations and people, and even thought the same of the Sadducees and most of the common people of their own nation. They were not considered the wealthy sect, but their ranks were blessed with noble teachers and religious leaders, among which were Nicodemus, Gamaliel, Joseph of Arimathea, and the Apostle Paul.

Conflict between John the Baptist and this sect was inevitable. One would certainly expect Jesus the Christ to have increasing conflict with the Pharisees, for He consistently rebuked and condemned them for the way they lived and taught the people, as referred to in many places in the Gospels, especially in Matthew 23:1-7; Mark 7:7; and Matthew 15:9. He rebuked them for "teaching for doctrines the commandments of men," and emphatically declared in Matthew 5:20 ". . .except your righteousness shall exceed the righteousness of the scribes and Pharisees, ye shall in no case enter into the kingdom of heaven."

Sadducee

The Sadducees were a sect or party of high priests, wealthy, influential and aristocratic families, most of whom were ready to embrace Hellenic culture. Formed also in the early part of the second century B.C., this sect was the most influential religious society in the economic and political life of Palestine, though not the most religiously inclined. Many of them were members of the Jewish high tribunal, the Sanhedrin.

While they rejected the oral laws and traditions of the Pharisees, the Sadducees clung to the written law of Moses, usually severe in its prosecution. They did not believe in a resurrection, nor in the immortality of the soul, nor in angels, feeling there was no basis for such beliefs. To them temple worship and sacrifice were uppermost and supreme, and they regarded the synagogue worship of the Pharisees dangerous to their national religion and the overall aspects of temple worship of Judaism as recommended by the law of Moses.

They were unpopular with the common people whom, it seems, they shunned except when it was advantageous for them. The Roman rulers held them in high esteem as a rule, since they influenced the control of the Jewish people. They held conservative views of the written law and judged accordingly. Because of the vast difference Jesus had much less to say of them than of the Pharisees, though He assailed them along with the Pharisees as mentioned by Matthew 16:6-12. They are mentioned also in Acts 4:1; 5:17; 23:6-8. They conspired in the crucifixion of Jesus, the death of James, and the death of Stephen, besides Peter's imprisonment.

This sect apparently disappeared with the destruction of Jerusalem in A.D. 70, and, it seems, never rose to prominence again.

Objective: The individual will demonstrate an understanding of the *background* of the Bible by locating the following geographical regions on a map of the world: Egypt, Palestine, Assyria, Babylonia, Persia, Asia Minor.

Ancient Near East

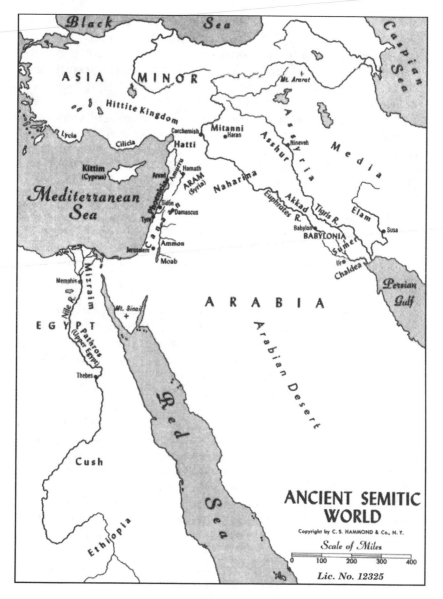

ANCIENT SEMITIC WORLD

Copyright by C. S. HAMMOND & Co., N. Y.

Scale of Miles
0   100   200   300   400

Lic. No. 12325

Objective: The individual will demonstrate an understanding of the *background* of the Bible by locating major cities, provinces, and bodies of water on a map of Palestine.

Bible Training Institute, Lessons in Bible Training, *Vol. II, pp. 5-7*

The known world of Christ's day was a relatively narrow strip of land encircling the Mediterranean Sea. It stretched from the Rock of Gibraltar in southern Spain eastward through Persia to the gates of India and thence on around the southern shore of the Mediterranean until it reached that point of Africa across the Straits of Gibraltar.

The main geographical subdivisions of the ancient world are as follows: On the northern coast of the Mediterranean were Rome, Greece, the Provinces of Asia Minor, and Syria; on the east coast of the Mediterranean was Palestine, and to the west of that, the expanse of land called Persia; on the southern shore of the Mediterranean from east to west were the nation of Egypt and the great expanse of Africa proper.

Of the most importance to our story is the geography of Palestine, the home of the human Christ. It is in the setting of this small country where the jewel of Christ's life was placed.

Provinces. Palestine was divided into five separate provinces; however, it is impossible to think of these provinces as having had fixed boundaries such as the states of the United States or as do most of the countries of the world in which we live. These boundaries varied so much from year to year that it is impossible now to fix exactly the provinces' areas.

Judea was the largest of these provinces. Roughly, it covered the territory which was originally allotted to the ancient tribes of Judah, Benjamin, Dan, and Simeon. It was bounded on the west by the Mediterranean Sea, on the south by the desert, on the east by the Dead Sea and the Jordan River, while Samaria was at its northern boundary.

Galilee was the northernmost province of the country of Palestine. It was bounded by the River Jordan and the Sea of Galilee to the east, by Samaria on the south, and Phoenicia on

---

From Bible Training Institute, *Lessons in Bible Training,* Vol. II, (Cleveland, TN: White Wing, 1976) pp. 5-7. Used by permission.

the north. The upper part of Galilee was rather mountainous while the lower was hilly, but very fertile. The inhabitants of this province were almost entirely Jewish, although many Gentiles lived in various places.

Perea and *Decapolis* were the other two provinces. While they are not as important to the story as the other three provinces, yet they do appear. Perea was directly east of Samaria and Judea, and embraced the territory originally belonging to the ancient tribes of Reuben and Gad. It is located east of the Jordan. Decapolis (which is a Greek word meaning "ten cities") gets its name from the ten cities of that area. This province is also east of the Jordan and the Sea of Galilee, but lies north of Perea.

Rivers and Lakes. Practically the only river of importance in the country of Palestine is the River Jordan. However, if it were not for the great event which took place around this river, it probably today would not enjoy much fame.

The Jordan River had its source high in the mountains north of Galilee and flowed south to empty into the Dead Sea, passing on its way through the Sea of Galilee. As it flowed south, it gradually cut a deeper and deeper canyon for itself until by the time it reached the Dead Sea, the level of the river was far below the level of the Mediterranean Sea. The land along its banks, for the most part, was relatively swampy but very, very fertile. It formed a natural boundary between several of the provinces of Palestine.

The Dead Sea is so named because there is no living thing in it or around it. It is a tremendously salty sea which receives the waters of the Jordan as they flow southward. The Sea of Galilee lies considerably north of the Dead Sea and is part of the boundary which separates the province of Galilee from the province of Decapolis. Its waters abounded in fish and its shores were very fertile.

Mountains. Extending southward from Syria through Palestine is a range of mountains known as the Lebanons. These are the most important mountains to our study. Probably the most important of the mountain peaks in this range are:

Mount of Transfiguration (or Mount Hermon). Mount Hermon is located in the province of Decapolis, quite a distance north of the Sea of Galilee.

The site of the *Sermon on the Mount* (or Mount Hittin). Mount Hittin is located in lower Galilee, west of the Sea.

In addition to these two mountains, of course, are the low peaks on which the city of Jerusalem was built and the *Mount of Olives* nearby.

Cities. The important cities of the life of Christ are relatively small in number. Foremost of these, of course, are:

Jerusalem, which was the center of the Jewish religion and was the actual scene of the sacrifice of the Son of God for the sins of the world.

Bethlehem, the birthplace of Christ, which was located south of Jerusalem in the province of Judea.

Nazareth in the hilly section of Galilee where Christ spent His boyhood days.

Capernaum, the seaport of the Sea of Galilee, where Christ made His headquarters for His Galilean ministry and where many of His disciples were called.

Objective: The individual will demonstrate an understanding of the background of the Bible by identifying the significance of the following people from the Intertestamental Period: Alexander the Great, Ptolemy, Antiochus Epiphanes, Mattathias, Judas Maccabeus, Pompey, and Herod the Great.

Bible Training Institute, General Bible Study, pp. 103-107

The period between Malachi and Matthew was a time of great change, featuring many political and imperial upheavals. It saw the rise and fall of several great empires and prepared the way for the first coming of the Son of God. Each event, as it is viewed across such great spans of time, bears a special relationship toward making ready for the advent of Christ. God's hand can be seen upon the scene of history, moving in mighty and mysterious ways His wonders to perform.

Fall of Persia. For approximately two hundred years the Persian empire ruled supremely among the nations of the Orient. But during the last few years of this supremacy, a great world conqueror was growing up in the mountain fortresses of Macedonia. This man, Alexander the Great, became the greatest military genius the world has ever known, who, before he had even reached maturity, had conquered nearly all the known world. The great Persian empire fell before his irresistible onslaught in the battle of Arbela in 330 B.C.

Rise and Fall of the Grecian Empire. Alexander continued his conquest and went all the way to India before turning to rest upon his laurels. He built a great empire based entirely

---

Bible Training Institute, *Lessons in Bible Training,* (White Wing)

upon his own iron will and the loyalty of his fighting men. The empire was held together by this one man; but when he died, the empire fell to pieces as if the string which binds together a bunch of sticks had been cut. After his death there was a period of warring and strife among his generals. Finally five of them set up separate kingdoms within the area of the empire of Alexander. These five engaged in constant warfare with each other, resulting in the downfall of two of the five. Those remaining were the kings of Macedonia, Syria-Palestine, and Egypt. The latter two are the only ones which need concern us in this study.

Ptolemies. In Egypt the great Greek general Ptolemy and his successors ruled over that land from Alexander's death to the time of the Roman conquests. They developed the great city of Alexandria and made Egypt practically the master of the Mediterranean Sea.

Seleucids. In Syria and the surrounding territories, Seleucus, another of Alexander's generals, became the ruler. At the time of his death he was bidding to reunite the Alexandrian empire under his rulership. His aspirations were defeated by his own death, and his son, Antiochus, was unable to carry them out to a successful conclusion. While the territory of this line of kings, known as the Seleucids, dwindled till little was left except Syria and Mesopotamia, it remained a power to be reckoned with in the Orient until the great tide of Roman conquest caught them as it had caught the rest of the civilized world.

Position of Palestine. The territory of Palestine, while not very large, was in a valuable geographic position. But this position also brought to bear upon it pressure from both the Ptolemies of Egypt and the Seleucids of Greek-Syria. Palestine was the corridor which afforded passage between the continents of Asia and Africa, providing the shortest possible route for both trading caravans and military forces. Thus, the Jews were caught in the pinch between the two continents, and in the course of the years between the death of Alexander and the Roman conquest, changed hands a number of times. Too, the battleground of the contending armies of these two ruling families was Palestine, which brought still more suffering to the Jews. It must be admitted, though, that the Ptolemies were very lenient and easy when the country was under their control, since they cared for nothing except the tribute money, and never attempted to interfere in the Jews' political, social, and religious life. With the Seleucids it was a different story, however, as we shall see.

The Maccabean Revolt. Several Seleucid rulers succeeded the original Seleucus on the throne of Greek-Syria. When Palestine was not under the control of one of the Ptolemies, it was squirming beneath the thumb of one of the Seleucids. All of these rulers were more or less tyrannical and made the Jews' lot a hard one. But the worst of them all was reserved till near the end of the Greek domination.

The Seleucid king most remembered by the Jews for his oppression and cruelty was called Antiochus Epiphanes. He launched a systematic program for the extermination of Judaism, seeking to replace it with the paganism of the Greeks. He proclaimed a decree forbidding all Jewish religious observances, which included fast days, the Sabbath, sacrifices, and circumcision. No one was to read the Mosaic law on pain of death. A huge army was sent to enforce the new law, arriving in Jerusalem on the Sabbath day, whereupon they practically destroyed the temple and enslaved many of the people. Adding insult to injury they set up a pagan altar to the worship of the Greek god Zeus, after having torn down the sacred sacrificial altar, and ordered the Jews to offer the flesh of swine as an offering to the heathen god.

By this time the loyal Jews were thoroughly aroused. They fled to the hills in huge numbers, banding together under the leadership of Mattahias, who led the people in guerrilla operations against the Syrians. When Mattahias died, he left the leadership of this motley army to his son Judas. Judas soon demonstrated his military ability and, due to his technique of constantly hammering at the enemy to wear him down, soon became known by the name of Maccabeus, which means the "Hammerer."

Finally awakening to the fact that he now had a full-scale rebellion on his hands, Antiochus decided to crush it once and for all. He sent an army into the hills, which he felt would subdue the upstart Maccabeus and beat the resistance completely, but the foxy Judas, who had a flair for military maneuvers, surprised the Syrian army in a narrow pass and utterly routed the troops, sending them fleeing for home. But Antiochus was a persistent soul. Not to be discouraged by the first defeat, Antiochus sent army after army into that wild terrain of northern Palestine to attempt the subjugation of the wily Maccabeus, only to be met and cut to pieces by the hard-fighting Jewish guerrillas. At length, realizing the seriousness of the situation, this Seleucid king ordered an army of 65,000 of his finest troops to march into the guerrilla territory to bring Judas Maccabeus to terms. The route of march made it necessary for the Syrians to go through a fairly narrow pass, whereupon Judas, with only one-sixth of their number, swooped down upon this huge force, completely bewildering the troops of Antiochus and sending them, too, scurrying for home.

Judas marched triumphantly into Jerusalem and set out to clean up the city, breaking down and destroying all the pagan idols which Antiochus had ordered erected in his program of making pagans out of Jews. After this wholesale housecleaning, they rededicated the temple. This was the Feast of the Dedication observed during the time of Jesus (John 10:22). The outcome of Judas' fight was the granting, to the Jews, of religious freedom, and Judas Maccabeus is credited with having saved Judaism from the throes of pagan worship. An independent government was set up which remained in force for approximately 128 years, ruled over by a line of kings known as the Maccabeans. In reality, these kings held the official title of high priest, and only a few of them took the title of king.

Rise of Rome. During the years of the early Maccabean struggles a new world power was rising in the west. The iron rule of the Romans was being gradually extended toward the east. Territory after territory fell before the all-conquering Roman armies. One by one the Greek kingdoms were absorbed into the ever-growing flood tide of Roman supremacy.

Conquest of Palestine. The Seleucid kingdom soon fell and with it the Romans received the territory of Palestine. During the rise of Roman power, the Maccabean rulers—ruling as high priests—were extending the borders of the Jewish province, and were continually mixed up in intrigues and fighting among themselves. When Pompey, the Roman general, appeared on the scene of Palestine in 63 B.C., he found a contest for the throne between two brothers of the Maccabean family, one of which was being supported by Antipater, the son of the governor of Idumea. Pompey, in acting as mediator, decided in favor of Hyrcanus, the favorite of Antipater, setting him up as high priest of the Jews.

Herods. In the ensuing few years, the family of the Idumean, Antipater, began to gain power in Palestine. This was the beginning of the rise to prominence of the family to be known as the Herods during the time of Christ. They courted the favor of the Romans, and eventually, in 40 B.C., Herod the Great, son of Antipater, was formally recognized by the Roman Senate as king of the Jews. This officially extinguished the rule of the Maccabeans which had been in force for around 128 years.

Herod returned from his successful trip to Rome and began a vigorous military campaign to capture Jerusalem. While thus engaged, he married Mariamne, the heiress of the Maccabean family, thus uniting the Idumean family of Herod with the Jewish family. The sons of Herod the Great were the rulers of Palestine at the time of Christ. Herod the Great was king of the territory when Christ was born; it was he who was visited by the wise men and who ordered the death of the babies of Bethlehem. He died very soon after the flight of Christ's family to Egypt and, by official Roman action, the country was divided among Herod's three sons—Herod Archelaus, Herod Antipas, and Herod Philip—who became known as tetrarchs.

Objective: The individual will demonstrate an understanding of the background of the Bible by identifying traditional authors of the books of the Bible

Bible Training Institute, General Bible Study, *pp. 13, 14, 109, 110*

The first major division is known as the **Pentateuch or Books of the Law.** "Pentateuch" is a Greek word meaning "five law books." The books included in this classification are:

1. Genesis, meaning "beginning."
2. Exodus, meaning "going out."
3. Leviticus, meaning "Levitical Book."
4. Numbers, so-called because it records the census of Israel.

Bible Training Institute, *General Bible Study,* (Cleveland, TN: White Wing, 1976). Used by permission.

5. Deuteronomy, meaning "two tables" or "two commandments."

These books are generally ascribed to Moses. Genesis has as part of its heading in the Authorized Version, "The First Book of Moses," and the other books of the Pentateuch have the same notation in numerical sequence.

The second division is known as the **Books of History**. These books deal primarily with the history of the Jewish nation from the conquests of Joshua to the rebuilding of the walls of Jerusalem by Nehemiah. They include the following:

1. Joshua, probably written by Joshua
2. Judges, author unknown
3. Ruth, author unknown
4. 1 Samuel, author unknown
5. 2 Samuel, author unknown
6. 1 Kings, Jewish tradition names Jeremiah as author
7. 2 Kings
8. 1 Chronicles, author uncertain, but probably Ezra
9. 2 Chronicles
10. Ezra, probably written by Ezra
11. Nehemiah, written by Nehemiah (Many students consider it his autobiography.)
12. Esther, author unknown.

The **Books of Poetry** comprise the next division. These books are considered the best of Jewish poetical expression, and literary experts universally praise them as some of the world's best literature. Under this heading are included:
1. Job, author unknown
2. Psalms, written by David and others. (Seventy-three Psalms have been attributed to David, although others of these poems may also have been written by him.)
3. Proverbs, written almost entirely by Solomon
4. Ecclesiastes, or The Preacher, also attributed to Solomon
5. Song of Songs, Song of Solomon, or Canticles, of which tradition names Solomon as the author

The next two sections are made up of the **Books of Prophecy**. The first of these sections includes the **Major Prophets**:

1. Isaiah
2. Jeremiah
3. Lamentations
4. Ezekiel
5. Daniel

All of these books, with the exception of Lamentations, bear the name of the author. Lamentations is generally accepted as having been written by Jeremiah.

There are twelve Books of the **Minor Prophets**. These are called minor, not necessarily because they are less important, but because of the comparatively short length of the books. They are:

1. Hosea
2. Joel
3. Amos
4. Obadiah
5. Jonah
6. Micah
7. Nahum
8. Habakkuk
9. Zephaniah
10. Haggai
11. Zechariah
12. Malachi

All these books, with the possible exception of Jonah, were written by the men whose names they bear. However, it is quite possible that Jonah did write the book which bears his name.

The New Testament is a compilation of twenty-seven books written in the hundred-year period from the birth of Christ to the death of John the Revelator about A.D. 98. They were written in the Greek language which shows definitely the influence of the period of the Greek supremacy in Palestine which has been studied. . . . The books fall into five natural classifications according to the nature of the book.[15]

The first four books are popularly known as the Gospels and are classed under the head of **Biography**. Matthew, Mark, and Luke, known as the Synoptic Gospels due to a great many points of similarity in their stories, were written by the men whose names they bear, sometime between the years A.D. 58 and A.D. 65. The Gospel of John was written between A.D. 90 and A.D. 98 by John the Beloved, apostle of Christ and the same man recorded Revelation.

The Acts of the Apostles, which records the history of the Early Church from the day of Pentecost to just prior to the martyrdom of the Apostle Paul, was written by Luke just a short time after the writing of his gospel. It is classed as **History**, being the only New Testament book under that heading.

The next group is called the **Pauline Epistles**, which consists of thirteen books or letters written by the Apostle Paul between the years A.D. 52 and A.D. 66. Under this major heading are several subdivisions into which the books are further classified. The first group we shall call *Early Epistles to the Churches*. It includes 1 and 2 Thessalonians (written first), Galatians, 1 and 2 Corinthians, and Romans. The second group, known as *Prison Epistles*, was written during his imprisonment in Caesarea and Rome. They are Philippians, Ephesians, Colossians, and Philemon; 1 and 2 Timothy and Titus are placed under the heading of *Pastoral Epistles*, although they also were written during Paul's sojourn under Roman care.

The next major division of the New Testament books is the **General Epistles**, so-called because they are not addressed to any specific church or individual, but were written to the entire Church at large. The first is Hebrews; the remaining books bear the names of their authors and are James; 1 and 2 Peter; 1, 2, and 3 John; and Jude.

The remaining division in the New Testament is that of **Prophecy** in which there is only one book, Revelation. This book, also called the Apocalypse, was written by the same John who wrote the other four books bearing his name in the New Testament. It was written during his banishment on the Isle of Patmos, sometime just prior to his death in A.D. 98.

The Content of the Old Testament

Unit Four

Objectives:

The individual will demonstrate an understanding of the *content* of the Old Testament by:

- identifying the theme, and where appropriate, the key events and people of each book of the Old Testament.
- constructing a chronological outline of the main events in the history of the people of Israel.
- describing the life and significance of the following people: Abraham, Isaac, Jacob, Joseph, Moses, Joshua, Samuel, Saul, David, Solomon, Isaiah, Jeremiah, Ezekiel, Nehemiah, Daniel.
- describing the significance of the following events: the call of Abraham, the exodus from Egypt, the establishment of the covenant at Sinai, the institution of the Levitical sacrifices, the conquest of Canaan, the rule by judges, the establishment of the monarchy, the division of the kingdom, the exile in Babylon, the return from captivity.
- naming the Ten Commandments.

Resource Guide for Learning Goals and Objectives

UNIT FOUR: THE CONTENT OF THE OLD TESTAMENT

Objective: The individual will demonstrate an understanding of the content of the Old Testament by constructing a chronological outline of the main events in the history of the people of Israel.

Bible Training Institute, General Bible Study, pp. 28, 39, 53, 65, 89

From Abraham to Moses

I. Abraham, Father of the Faithful
  A. Lot and Early Life of Abraham
  B. Isaac, the Son of Promise

II. Israel and His Family
  A. Laban and the Years of Labor
  B. Joseph, the Dreamer
  C. Joseph in Egypt

III. Israel in Egypt
  A. World Famine
  B. Land of Goshen
  C. Oppression and Early Years of Moses

IV. Moses and the Deliverance
  A. Call of Moses
  B. Plagues in Egypt
  C. Exodus

V. Wandering in the Wilderness
  A. To Mount Sinai
    1. Pillar of Cloud and Fire (Exod. 13:20-22)
    2. Manna Given (16:4-15)
    3. Ten Commandments Given (19:16-20:21)
    4. Worship of the Golden Calf (ch. 32)
  B. Wandering After Mount Sinai
    1. First Numbering of Israel (Num. 1:1-4, 46, 47)
    2. Manna and the Quails (11:1-33)
    3. Rebellion of Miriam and Aaron (12:1-16)
    4. Sending of Twelve Spies (ch. 13;14)
    5. Rebellion of Korah (ch. 16)

(Note: There is a break in the story here, which is not resumed until chapter 20, picking up the history 38 years later.)

From Bible Training Institute, General Bible Study, (Cleveland, TN: White Wing, 1976). Used by permission.

C. Later Years of Wandering
1. Plague of Serpents (Num. 21:5-9)
2. Conquest of Gilead and Bashan (21:21-35)
3. Balaam (ch. 22-24)
4. Second Census (26:1-51)
5. Joshua Anointed (27:15-23)
6. Conquest of the Midianites (31:1-12)
7. Death of Moses on Mount Nebo (Deut. 34)

From Joshua to Saul

I. Period of Conquest
   A. Conquests West of the Jordan—Joshua (Book of Joshua.)
   B. Other Conquests—Judah and other tribes (Judges 1, 2:1-10)

II. Period of the Judges
   A. Conditions in Canaan
   B. History of Important Judges
      1. Othniel, the First Judge
      2. Ehud, the Left-handed Judge
      3. Deborah, the Woman Judge
      4. Gideon and the Famous Three Hundred
      5. Jephthah, Who Made a Rash Vow
      6. Samson, the Strong Man
      7. Eli, Who Lost the Ark
   C. Samuel, the Last and Greatest Judge (1 Samuel)
      1. Early Life
      2. The Reign of Saul, the First King
      3. Early Life of David

From David to the Captivity

I. Reign of David (2 Samuel; 1 Kings 1; 2:1-11; 1 Chron. 11-19)
   A. Personal Life
   B. Military Campaigns
   C. David and Prophecy
II. Reign of Solomon (1 Kings 1-11; 1 Chron. 28, 29; 2 Chron. 1-9)
   A. Solomon's Personal Life
   B. The Temple

III. Division of the Kingdom (1 Kings 12-22; 2 Kings; 2
Chron. 10-36)
A. Israel
1. Kings
2. Prophets
3. Assyrian Conquest and Captivity
B. Judah
1. Kings
2. Babylonian Conquest and Captivity

Minor Prophets and Return From Exile

I. Kingdom or Pre-Captivity Prophets
A. Judah
1. Joel
2. Micah
3. Nahum
4. Habakkuk
5. Zephaniah
B. Israel
1. Jonah
2. Amos
3. Hosea

II. Captivity
A. Obadiah
B. Others

III. Return From Exile
A. Important Historical Figures
B. Restoration or Post-Captivity Prophets
1. Haggai and Zechariah
2. Malachi

Objective: The individual will demonstrate an understanding
of the content of the Old Testament by describing the life and
significance of the following people: Abraham, Isaac, Jacob,
Joseph, Moses, Joshua, Samuel, Saul, David, Solomon, Isaiah,
Jeremiah, Ezekiel, Nehemiah, Daniel.

Abraham, Father of the Faithful. (1996-1822 B.C.) God's word came first to Abram in Ur of the Chaldees. Abram and his family started out for the land of promise, but got only as far as Haran[16] where they must have lived for several years, until Terah died (Gen. 12:5).

Sojourn in Egypt (Gen. 12:10-20). Abram, with his entire household, moved on into Canaan, where the Lord promised him the entire region for him and his seed forever. However, at that time a great famine was in the land, so he journeyed on southward into Egypt, where he remained for a while. Fearing that Sarai's beauty would enflame the men of Egypt to kill him to possess her, he told them she was his sister. Unaware that this was only a partial truth, the Pharaoh had her taken into his harem. However, the Lord appeared to Pharaoh and warned him of the real relationship of Abram and Sarai, whereupon the Egyptian monarch became vexed at Abram and requested his immediate departure.

Contention With Lot (Gen. 13:5-18). Up to this time Abram and Lot, his nephew, had not been separated. They had traveled and dwelled together. But there began to be quarrels among the herdsmen over the grazing land, since both men's flocks had grown to enormous size. In order to avoid any real trouble, Abram proposed to Lot that they separate, giving Lot the first choice of land. Lot chose the fertile plains of the Jordan and pitched his tents toward the wicked city of Sodom, and Abram moved on south, settling in the region of Hebron.

Melchizedek (Gen. 14:1-24). Shortly after the separation of Lot and Abram, Chedorlaomer, the king of Elam, together with three other kings, made war on the land of Sodom and Gomorrah. In the course of the fighting Sodom and Gomorrah were routed, and Lot, with all his goods, was taken captive. Abram heard the news from an escaped captive, immediately armed his household, and went in pursuit. He fell upon the marauders, utterly defeating them, not only freeing the captives, but taking much spoil from the defeated army. On his return he met the mysterious Melchizedek, King of Salem. This godly priest-like figure so impressed Abram that he gave to him a

---

From Bible Training Institute, *Genral Bible Study,* (Cleveland, TN: White Wing, 1976) pp. 30-98. Used by permission.

tenth of all he had taken. This is the first recorded instance of the tithe being paid.[17]

Hagar and Ishmael (Gen. 16:3-14; 21:9-21). Sarai, certain that her barrenness would prevent her from giving birth to a son, prevailed upon Abram to have a child by Hagar, her Egyptian handmaid. When it was certain that Hagar was with child, Sarai saw immediately that Hagar despised her because of her barrenness, no doubt feeling superior to her mistress. Sarai's persecution of Hagar then drove her from the household. However, the Lord appeared to Hagar and instructed her to return to her mistress, telling her that her son would be very wild and warlike. When the child was born, he was named Ishmael. Several years later, when Isaac was being weaned, the mockery of Ishmael caused Sarai to entreat Abram to send him and his mother away. Abram did so only after the Lord had promised to make of Ishmael also a great nation. Ishmael and his mother dwelt in the wilderness where the boy became an archer and eventually took himself an Egyptian wife.

Sodom and Gomorrah (Gen. 18-19:29). One day as Abraham[18] sat in the door of his tent, three strangers appeared. Abraham, recognizing at once their divine nature, treated them with all the honor and hospitality possible. In the course of conversation, Abraham learned of the pending destruction of Sodom and Gomorrah. Abraham began pleading for the salvation of the city for the sake of the righteous dwelling within its walls. After a long plea to the Lord, Abraham finally received the Lord's promise to spare the city if ten righteous persons could be found there. However, apparently there were not even ten righteous people there for the Lord sent angels to warn Lot and his family to flee before they rained destruction upon the city. Lot, his wife, and two daughters fled the city, having been warned not to look back; and as they fled, God rained fire and brimstone upon the whole plain where Sodom was, utterly destroying it. Lot's wife could not refrain from disobeying the word of God, looked back, and became a pillar of salt.[19]

Birth of Isaac (Gen 21:1-8). Up until now, Sarah had never had a child. She was growing old, much past the age of child bearing. But God had promised Abraham an heir; and, although Sarah had once laughed at the promise, they now believed and looked forward to it in their old age (Heb. 11:11). So, Sarah conceived and bore a child in Abraham's one-hundredth year, calling him Isaac, which means "laughter." And, in obedience to the command of God, he took Isaac and circumcised him on the eighth day as a token of the covenant between God and Abraham.

Sacrifice of Isaac (Gen. 22:2-14). The story of the sacrifice of Isaac is very familiar—how God told Abraham to present his son as an offering to the Lord and how Abraham doubted not the goodness of God and prepared Isaac for the sacrifice. But as the sacrificial knife was descending, God stayed the hand of Abraham, having provided a ram caught in the bushes to substitute for Isaac on the altar.[20]

Death of Sarah (Gen. 23). Sarah died in Hebron when she was one hundred twenty-seven years old. She was buried in the cave of the field of Machpelah before Mamre, which Abraham had bought from Ephron the Hittite for four hundred shekels of silver. This cave was to be a very important burial place for the chosen family in later years.

Isaac and Rebekah (Gen. 24:1-67). Abraham desired that Isaac should have a wife before he, Abraham, should die. So, he sent his servant Eliezer (15:2) to the land of his kinsmen in Haran to find Isaac a wife from among his own people. Eliezer reached the city of Nahor, Abraham's brother. There he asked the Lord to show him the woman God would have for Isaac. He would know the woman because she would not only give him to drink from the well, but would water his camels also. The woman who fulfilled the promise was Rebekah, granddaughter of Abraham's brother. In the course of events, she was taken back to Canaan to be the wife of Isaac.

Death of Abraham (Gen 25:7-10). Abraham lived to see Isaac married. When he was one hundred seventy-five years old, he died and was buried in the cave with Sarah. Thus passed one of the most important men in history, both to the Jews and the Christians. To him was the first great promise given and through him was every people of the earth to be blessed. He is mentioned seventy-four times in the New Testament! Notice these: (1) the seed of Abraham (John 8:31-44, Rom. 9); (2) doctrine of justification by faith, (Rom. 4; Gal. 3:6-18); (3) allegory of Hagar and Sarah, (Gal. 4:21-31); (4) faith of Abraham (Heb. 11:8-19); (5) faith plus works (James 2:20-26). Also, here is a list of Scripture references to the promises given to Abraham: Gen. 12:1-3, 7; 13:14-17; 15:1-21; 17:1-22; 22:15-18. Abraham's change of names has been mentioned. Notice that Sarah's name also was changed (Gen. 17:15).

Isaac, the Son of Promise. (1896-1717 B.C.) A great deal of Isaac's story has been told in connection with the life of Abraham. Abraham died at the age of one hundred seventy-five, Isaac then being seventy-five years old.

Birth of Esau and Jacob (Gen. 25:24-28). In response to Rebekah's petition because of her barrenness, God answered. When the time came that she should be delivered, they were twins. The first child born was Esau, called this because he was very hairy.[21] Jacob, which means "supplanter," was the second child. (See the section on Jacob or Israel.)

The Wells (Gen. 26). God renewed with Isaac the promise he had given to Abraham. Isaac has been called the "Son of Promise." He went to Gerar to live, where he became wealthy, owner of great flocks. He was envied by the Philistines, who filled up the wells that Abraham had dug. Isaac was forced to move often, stopping frequently to dig again the wells of his father, but everywhere it was necessary to contend with the Philistines. Finally, he found a peaceful place at Beersheba, where he settled, having discovered a well of "springing water."

Deception of Jacob (Gen. 27). Isaac became blind in his later years. His favorite son was Esau, because this son was the hunter and supplied his father with venison, his favorite dish. At last he called Esau to him to prepare him some venison, and when he would bring it to him, he would give him his blessing. However, in the well-known trick, Jacob deceived Isaac and received the blessing instead.

Remainder of Isaac's life (Gen. 28:1-9; 35:27-29). Of the remainder of his life we know little, with the exception of a few isolated facts. Not desiring that Jacob should marry a Canaanite wife—as Esau had done—Isaac sent him away to Padan-aram to seek a wife among his kinsmen there. He was still alive when Jacob returned from the house of Laban about twenty-one years later. He died not long thereafter at the age of one hundred eighty, both Jacob and Esau being there to bury him.

Israel and His Family. (Jacob lived from 1839 to 1689 B.C.) We pick up history on the way to Padan- aram or Haran, to take a wife from among his mother's people. On his way, he stopped at a place to sleep (Gen. 28:10-22). He dreamed of a ladder between earth and heaven, upon which the angels were descending and ascending. Above the ladder, the Lord stood and renewed with Jacob the promises which He had made with Abraham and with Isaac. When Jacob awoke, he set up a stone for a pillar, anointed it with oil, and called the spot where he had slept, Bethel, which means "the house of God."

Labors for Laban (Gen. 29:1-30). When Jacob arrived at Haran, he fell in love with Rachel, the younger daughter of Laban, his mother's brother. He contracted to give Laban seven years of labor in exchange for the hand of his daughter. However, at the end of the seven years, he was tricked into marrying Leah, the older daughter. So, he was forced to work another seven years for Rachel. After that, he worked another six years amassing great flocks of sheep and goats. Then he left the household of Laban to go back to Canaan.

Birth of Joseph (Gen. 30:1-24). During the later years of his labors, there had been born several children to Jacob. Reuben, Simeon, Levi, Judah, Issachar, and Zebulun were the sons of Leah; Gad and Asher were born to Zilpah, Leah's handmaid; Dan and Naphtali were the sons of Bilhah, Rachel's handmaid. Rachel was barren for a long time, but finally she gave birth to a son and called him Joseph, which means "adding." The son became one of the greatest figures in world history.

Wrestling with the Lord (Gen. 32:22-32). On his way back to Canaan, Jacob had an odd experience. Being left alone one evening he became engaged in a wrestling match with a mysterious man. All night long they wrestled, for Jacob would not let him go until the man blessed him. The man did bless him, giving him the name of Israel, which means "a prince of God." Jacob named that place Peniel—"the face of God"—because he had seen God face to face.

Meeting with Esau (Gen. 33:1-20). Jacob had sent on ahead of him gifts of appeasement for Esau, because he feared his brother's anger was still strong against him. However, the meeting was one of glad reunion, Esau receiving him in a forgiving spirit. They parted on good terms and Jacob journeyed on, stopping eventually before the city of Shechem.

Birth of Benjamin (Gen. 35:16-20). On the way from Bethel—where Jacob had gone in response to the call of God—to Ephrath (Bethlehem), Rachel gave birth to another son, but did not live to see him; she died in childbirth. His father named him Benjamin.

Remainder of Jacob's life (Gen. 35:22-50:3). The rest of the life of Jacob is not recorded in detail. All that we know of it will be told along with the story of Joseph and his adventures in Egypt.

Joseph. He was the elder son of Rachel and Jacob, born before Jacob left the house of Laban. His only full brother was Benjamin, his mother dying at his birth. The first important mention of Joseph was when he was seventeen years old (Gen. 37). It is an old familiar story how Joseph was the favorite of his father and envied by his brothers, how he dreamed of his brothers bowing down and worshiping him, and how they sold him to traders on their way to Egypt. Reuben and Judah were not willing that they should kill him, as some of them desired, but Judah had suggested his sale to the Midianites.

Adventures in Egypt (Gen. 39; 40). Once in Egypt, Joseph was sold to Potiphar, the captain of Pharaoh's guard. By virtue of his fidelity to God and his Egyptian master, Potiphar made him overseer of all his house. However, Potiphar's wife, after having failed to get a response from Joseph to her shameless advances, in revenge convinced her husband that Joseph had attempted to violate his master's trust. As a consequence, Joseph was thrown into the royal prison. In prison Joseph gained a reputation as an interpreter of dreams. After two full years, Pharaoh began to have dreams which his magicians could not interpret. Then he heard of Joseph, whom he then brought from the prison that his dreams might be made known. The dreams were interpreted to mean that in Egypt there would be seven years of plenty followed by seven years of famine. He advised Pharaoh to store foodstuffs during the years of plenty, that the people might not perish during the lean years. Pharaoh, much impressed with the wisdom of Joseph, made him ruler over all Egypt, second to none save himself in trusting him with the storage project. Joseph was thirty years old when he received this royal appointment.

Israel in Egypt (Gen. 41-44). The famine came, being very severe and widespread. It reached even unto Canaan, where Joseph's father and brethren dwelled. Eventually they heard of the great store in Egypt, and Israel sent his sons to buy grain. That story is very well-known. Eventually Joseph made himself known and sent for Israel and the entire household to move into Egypt. This they did, settling in the land of Goshen.[22]

Jacob blessed his sons (Gen. 46-49). Jacob lived in Goshen for seventeen years; and as he was dying, he called for Joseph to come. Israel blessed Ephraim and Manasseh, the two sons of Joseph. Contrary to the custom of the eastern peoples, he conferred the greatest blessing upon Ephraim, the younger, promising that his posterity would be great and would "become a multitude of nations." These two sons were to divide the inheritance of Joseph in the promised land. Jacob also called his other sons to confer upon them either his displeasure or his blessing. Thee of them—Reuben, Simeon, and Levi—had incurred his displeasure. These three received no blessing of their father. Judah received a special blessing, greater than any of his brethren, for it was from the tribe of Judah that the promised Messiah was to come (Gen. 49:8-12; read also the promise to Joseph, Gen. 49:22-26). Jacob died and all Egypt mourned his death. To fulfill the promise to Jacob that he would bury him with Abraham, Joseph assembled a great company, including all the house of Israel and the nobles of Egypt, to carry the body of Jacob back to Canaan. There they buried him in the cave with Abraham and Sarah.

Death of Joseph. (Gen. 50). Joseph died when he was one hundred ten years old. They embalmed him, but left him in Egypt. However, Joseph looked ahead to when the Israelites would be leaving Egypt, leaving a dying wish that his bones be carried along.

Oppression and Early Years of Moses (Exod. 1–2:25). The family of Israel was given the land of Goshen to inhabit, and here is where they lived during their sojourn in Egypt. Years passed and a new king arose over Egypt who oppressed the Hebrews severely, for he was unacquainted with Joseph and his great service to Egypt. He feared the great foreign people within his borders, reasoning that they might revolt against him. How long after Joseph that the oppression came is not known. Joseph lived in Egypt for ninety-three years, and the children of Israel were in Egypt about four hundred years (Acts 7:6). So it was somewhere near the end of this period that Moses lived.

Moses was born during a period of intensified oppression.[23] It was necessary for his mother to hide him, to escape the decree of the king that all male Hebrew children were to be killed at birth. The story of the basket among the bulrushes in the river and Moses' childhood in the royal palace is universally known. Moses was to have a special part on God's program; therefore, it was imperative that he be saved. For forty years Moses lived as a member of the royal family of Egypt, but he knew of his Hebrew origin. Seeing one of his own race being mistreated by an Egyptian, he killed the Egyptian, and as a consequence, was forced to flee. He fled to the wilderness of Midian, where he lived another forty years.

Moses and the Deliverance (Exod. 3-14). Called into the presence of the Lord by the startling sight of the burning bush, Moses was instructed that the time for deliverance had come. Immediately he began making excuses, to the extent that God became angry with him.[24] Finally, after repeated promises from God, Moses started for Egypt.

Return to Egypt (Exod. 5:1-7:7). However, Pharaoh was not ready to let the people go. Plague after plague God sent upon the land of Egypt and still the heart of Pharaoh was like a stone. But at last came the plague of death to the firstborn in every house of Egypt, which brought the Pharaoh and all his people to beg the Israelites to leave the country.[25]

Exodus (Exod. 12:37-14:31). The children of Israel gathered up their flocks, herds, and their family belongings and began to trek out of Egypt, the men alone numbering over 600,000 strong. The first leg of their journey was from Rameses, the great treasure city they had built as slaves of Pharaoh, to Succoth on the shore of the Red Sea. However, by divine influence, Pharaoh changed his mind, gathered his army and started in pursuit of the fleeing people. Then it was that the Lord opened the way through the sea and closed it again to destroy the pursuing Egyptian army. This was only the beginning of God's great favor and care of His chosen people, although Israel failed Him repeatedly.

Joshua—Period of Conquest. The period of the conquest of the Promised Land began under Moses on the east bank of the Jordan River, before they crossed over into the land of promise. Moses died on Mount Nebo, never having set foot on the promised soil. His successor, Joshua, was given the privilege of leading the people across and subduing the peoples who were then occupying the territory.

Conquests West of the Jordan (Josh. 6-10). Jericho was the first place to fall before the invading armies of Israel. Here it was that the famous marches around the walls took place. Jericho was a city whose only defense was her walls, and when these fell, as a result of Israel's obedience to God, destruction of the city was easy. The conquest of Ai was a little more difficult by reason of one man's disobedience. God had commanded that everything was to be destroyed, but Achan took a golden wedge and a foreign garment, hiding them in his tent. Thus, the first try to defeat Ai ended in failure. Finally, however, after Achan's crime was discovered and he was put to death, the victory was gained (Josh. 7; 8:1-29). The city of Gibeon made peace with Joshua and became the servants of the children of Israel. However, the kings of the south of Canaan conspired to conquer Gibeon to punish her for allying with the Israelites. Gibeon sent a plea to Joshua for aid; Joshua responded by gathering his troops, and in a quick march to the south, fell upon the allied kings utterly destroying them, with the help of a hailstorm sent upon the enemy by God. It was in this battle that the sun stood still in obedience to the command of Joshua (Josh. 10:1-24). While he was still in the south, Joshua, with amazing efficiency and trip-hammer speed, conquered many of the heathen cities. ". . . Joshua smote all the country of the hills, and of the south, and of the vale, and of the springs, and all their kings: he left none remaining, but utterly destroyed all that breathed, as the Lord God of Israel commanded" (Josh. 10:40).

Then in a quick thrust, he and his army marched almost to the gates of Zidon far to the north, destroying cities, armies, and kings as he went. With this northern campaign, the great task of subduing the peoples inhabiting the land was almost completed; and when the "land rested from war," Joshua began the great division of the inheritance as promised to the twelve tribes of Israel. However, although the main problem of conquest was over, there remained some small areas to occupy and a few warlike tribes to conquer. This conquest was not really complete until the time of David.

Samuel, the Last and Greatest Judge. The personal and public life of Samuel extends into the lifetime of both Saul and David. He is also known as the "kingmaker," having anointed both Saul and David as the kings approved by God for Israel. . . .

Samuel was the son of Elkanah and Hannah. Samuel's birth was God's answer to Hannah's prayer and her vow that she would give her son to the service of the Lord. She kept her vow, presenting him to Eli when she had weaned him. Thus it was that Samuel thought he heard the voice of Eli calling him, but discovered it was the voice of God telling him of the destruction which was coming to the house of Eli for the wickedness of his sons. This vision was also Samuel's call to be a prophet of the Lord. After Eli's death, Samuel judged all of Israel for the remainder of his life. All during his life, the Israelites had to contend with the Philistines, and, although Samuel was no warrior, they won many battles from them, for ". . .the hand of the Lord was against the Philistines all the days of Samuel" (1 Sam. 7:13).

When Samuel was old, he made his two sons judges of Israel. However, ". . .his sons walked not in his ways, but turned aside after lucre, and took bribes, and perverted judgment" (1 Sam. 8:3). Then the people came to Samuel and desired him to give them a king to rule over them.[26] Samuel was reluctant to do so, but he prayed about it. The Lord told him to yield to their demands, but to warn them that a king would oppress them and enslave them. Such a change in government was a transition from a theocracy— the reign of God—to a monarchy—the reign of one man. Samuel told the people the mind of God, but they were not willing to give up the idea of having a king.

The Reign of Saul. God's choice rested upon Saul, of the tribe of Benjamin. Saul was a giant of a man, standing head and shoulders above all the people (1 Sam. 9:2). At the time of his selection, he was also an humble man, a sincere worshiper of God. Saul, when he first met Samuel, was searching for his father's asses which were lost. He had come to Samuel in the hopes that the prophet might be able to tell him where they might be found. The Lord informed Samuel at this time that Saul was the man whom He had chosen to be the first king of Israel.

Saul was anointed by Samuel at Samuel's home, and from that time he possessed the God-given authority of kingship.

However, he was not formally recognized by the people as king until some time later at Mizpeh, where the people had gathered in response to the call of Samuel. There he received the popular recognition, and his recognition by God was made known to the people. But some people were still not satisfied. The final confirmation of his authority was made still later at Gilgal, after Saul had shown his military ability in defeating the Ammonites.

But Saul's humbleness did not last long. After two years of reign, he began to be exalted in his office and to disobey the commandments of the Lord. He presumed to offer a burnt sacrifice, which privilege was reserved solely for the priest. Thus, he incurred the displeasure of the Lord and began the slow process of the loss of his power. He won many great battles after this episode, but the days of his power were surely numbered, and as his disobedience increased, that power became less and less.

It would be impossible to cover every detail of the lives of Samuel, Saul, and David as it is outlined in the last few chapters of 1 Samuel. Only a few of the most important will be mentioned. Samuel, as spokesman for the Lord, told Saul to make war upon the Amalekites and utterly destroy every man, woman, child, and beast. Saul gathered his armies, went down to Amalek and won a brilliant victory. But, in disobedience to God's command, he spared Agag, the king of Amalek, along with the finest animals in the Amalekite herds, bringing these back as the spoils of victory. Samuel got wind of it and met Saul on the way back. Samuel rebuked Saul for his disobedience, informing him that God was sorry that He had chosen Saul, that God had rejected him from being king, and was going to choose another.[27] From that time on, the decline of Saul's power was very rapid.

David. At this point, the lives of Samuel, Saul, and David cross, and the study of any one of these men will inevitably involve a study of the other. Samuel was reaching the end of his old age, Saul's power was waning, and David's star was rising. Samuel went down to the household of Jesse to choose a successor for Saul. He reviewed before him the older sons of Jesse, but none of them was the choice of God. They sent for David, who was tending the sheep, and God's choice fell upon the young shepherd lad; and from the moment that Samuel's anointing oil flowed upon his head, the Spirit of God was upon him.

After the well-known battle in which David killed Goliath and the Philistines were routed because of God's favor upon David, the new hero of Israel made a triumphant return to his country. As he crossed the territory, from every city women came forth dancing and singing, "Saul hath slain his thousands, and David his ten thousands" (1 Sam. 18:7). The reports of this stirred the jealous heart of Saul, and henceforth Saul sought to destroy David, except at certain times when he needed David to play for him or to help him in battle.

It was during this difficult period that the friendship between Saul's son, Jonathan, and David blossomed into the wonderful relationship it was. The great love between these two is used over and over as one of the world's best examples of undying manly affection that could not be marred by family or political differences. No malice or ill-will blemished this perfect companionship, and it lasted even after death in the families of the two men.

The aging Prophet Samuel soon died, leaving Saul in a very shaky and insecure position as king. In a very short time after this, Saul was forced into battle with the Philistines. Before the battle, having lost access to Samuel's advice, he sought the witch of Endor that she might consult the spirit of the dead prophet to ascertain the outcome of the battle. The spirit of Samuel informed the trembling Saul that his throne was to be occupied by David and that he and his sons were to die in the battle with the Philistines. The prophecy came to pass, Saul and his three sons, including Jonathan, falling at Mount Gilboa (1 Sam. 31). Thus ended the reign of the first king of Israel.

Reign of David (2 Sam. 2-1 Kings 2). Immediately following the death of Saul, there was a period of confusion concerning the throne. Ishbosheth, Saul's son, reigned in Israel, and in Judah David sat upon the throne at Hebron. Civil war broke out between the rival houses for the throne, "but David waxed stronger and stronger, and the house of Saul waxed weaker and weaker" (2 Sam. 3:1). Ishbosheth was murdered in the second year of his reign—not at the instigation of David, however—and David ascended the throne of the entire country. For five and a half years thereafter David ruled from Hebron, but at the end of that time he moved his headquarters to Jerusalem, where he reigned the remainder of his life.

Personal Life (1 Sam. 18-2 Sam. 18). It will be remembered that the great friendship between David and Jonathan was discussed. After Jonathan's death in battle, David mourned over the loss of his friend. After David ascended the throne of the entire country, he made inquiries concerning Jonathan's family and discovered that one son was living. His name was Mephibosheth, a cripple, whom David immediately invited to share his material wealth and to reside at the royal residence. Thus, the great friendship went on after Jonathan's death in the person of his son.

It was mentioned above concerning David's mourning over the loss of Jonathan. It seems proper to emphasize the fact that David did not allow political alignments, the enmity of others, or the necessity for doing certain unpleasant tasks to destroy his sense of affection and pity. Notice that, although Saul had sought to kill him, David lamented loudly when he heard of the death of the "Lord's anointed" (2 Sam. 1). His own son Absalom once led a revolt against him and treated his father in a very ill manner. In the course of the fighting Absalom was killed, but despite the son's rebellion and animosity toward his father, David could not be consoled at the news of his death (2 Sam. 18:33). David was a warring man, but his heart was tender and easily touched by tragedy or another's misfortune.

But there is a dark side to David's life. David remained in Jerusalem once and sent Joab to lead the army out to battle. While they were gone, he saw the wife of Uriah, the Hittite, and desired to have her for himself. He sent word to Joab to have Uriah put at the very hottest point of the battle that he might be killed, in order to make his possession of Bathsheba easier. But this greatly displeased the Lord. He sent Nathan the prophet to inform David of His displeasure and to make him aware of the great sin which he had committed. David, when he saw that he had lost favor in God's eyes, immediately repented of his great evil and began to seek God's approval on his life. It is very noticeable in the life of David, that, although he committed great sins, he never failed to repent and acknowledge before God the error of his ways. Many of the Psalms are songs of repentance or of thanksgiving that his repentance had been accepted.

David desired greatly to build a temple that would be worthy of the God of Israel. However, God was not willing that the temple should be built by David since he was a man of war, and many people had been slain at his hand. The building of the temple was to be the undertaking of Solomon, the king's son (2 Sam. 7). However, David began gathering the material for the temple's erection, even though he knew that it would never be built during his life. He was very submissive to the will of God, and he wanted everything to be in readiness when the time came for the house of the Lord to go up (1 Chron. 22).

Military Campaigns (1 Sam. 30-2 Sam. 21). David was a mighty warrior, a capable general, and a great leader of men. His military exploits began even before he was enthroned as monarch, for he was one of Saul's field marshals before Saul's enmity was aroused. But David's conquests and military feats after his coronation gave the Jewish empire a firmly established foundation and completed the subjugation of the native peoples of Canaan land which had started under Moses.

The eighth chapter of 2 Samuel enumerates many of the great victories of David, the warrior. He fought against the Philistines and the Moabites, defeating them and making them his tributaries. David conducted a campaign to extend his borders to the Euphrates River, and in the process, fought and defeated the king of Zobah, capturing chariots, horses, and 20,700 soldiers. The Syrians quickly mobilized their forces and came down to give Zobah aid, but David, in a magnificent display of military strength, met the Syrian army and defeated it. As a result of this battle, Syria was made subject to Israel, and David sent an army of occupation into Damascus, their capital city.

These victories, along with several others catalogued in this chapter, made the name of David a terror to the outlying countries. His military prowess caused the nations to fear the now powerful little country of Israel. David's troops occupied several of the surrounding nations which had given a great deal of trouble to his predecessors.

Besides these conflicts with foreign nations, two civil revolts are of interest. The rebellion of Absalom has been mentioned. This insurrection was put down with dispatch, but not without some initial successes of Absalom's cause. By trickery Absalom had won to this side nearly the entire area of Israel, which was considerably larger than the area left to his father. His initial successes even enabled him to occupy Jerusalem, but Absalom's forces were finally routed, and he was killed by Joab. Another revolt arose, this time at the instigation of a Benjamite by the name of Sheba. Again the tribes of Israel were disloyal to the king, and, as before, the men of Judah remained loyal. The trouble stemmed from the jealousy of the ten tribes of Israel over Judah's part in conducting the king back to Jerusalem after the defeat of Absalom (2 Sam. 19:40-43). This rebellion was short-lived. Joab besieged Sheba in a city called Abel, where he was beheaded by the people of the city to prevent its destruction by David's army.

The last battle in which David personally participated was with the Philistines. In the press of battle, David fatigued quickly because of his age, and if one of his men had not been on hand, he would have been killed. His men became frightened at this prospect and vowed that David would no longer personally lead the army into battle where he might lose his life. Even though other battles were fought, David left their execution in the hands of his trustworthy and capable generals.

David and Prophecy (2 Sam. 22; Psalms). David is quite an important prophetic figure, both as a prophet and as the object of prophecy. His great position is even greater when we realize that Christ is a direct descendant. Several references are made, during the history of David's reign, to the eternal establishment of his house upon the throne of Israel. This is direct prophecy concerning the fact that Christ, the Son of David, would be the great King over the spiritual kingdom of Israel. Many are the references to David in the New Testament as the ancestor of Christ, as well as several references to his prophecies. (Several of the Psalms are prophetic. Examples are Psalms 22 and 110.)

Reign of Solomon. The reign of Solomon saw the height of Jewish power—saw the borders of the Jewish–state extended to its greatest area. The glory of Solomon's court was known the world over, and the wisdom of Solomon was noised about in every royal residence of the ancient world. (Witness the visit of the Queen of Sheba.)

Personal Life (1 Kings 1-3;10;11). The throne, by rights of an elder son, belonged to Adonijah. But David wanted

Solomon to have the crown, so he had him anointed king before his death. It is a well-known story how Solomon prayed to God for wisdom, how his prayers were answered, and how he became the wisest man of the ancient world. (For examples of his wisdom see 1 Kings 4:16-28.)

Solomon's one great fault was a weakness for women. He especially desired the women of foreign nations and, before he died, had brought one thousand women together in his household. This was very definitely against the precepts of God, who had said that the children of Israel were neither to bring strange women into their own households, nor to espouse the women of foreign nations in their homes. Nearly all of Solomon's wives were foreign women who still retained the worship of the gods of their native lands. Through their influence, Solomon turned aside to idolatry and began to offer incense to strange gods in the very capital of Jehovah worship. His alienation from the God of his forefathers was so complete that we can find no record that Solomon ever repented of his backsliding and returned to God before he died.

Solomon inherited the poetic nature of his father, although his poetry is not the deeply religious type so typical of the Psalmist David. Solomon, himself, was the author of two distinct poetic types: one exemplified by Proverbs and Ecclesiastes, the other type shown by the exuberant poetic expression in the Song of Solomon. (The difference between these two types can easily be seen by comparing these books.)

The Temple (1 Kings 4-9). While Solomon's public life cannot be entirely separated from his private affairs, a division of the two makes the study of his reign a little easier. The greatest single item in the reign of Solomon was the building of the temple. (Some discussion of this was made during the study of the personal life of David, in which the personal reasons why David could not build the temple were given. In Solomon's reign, the problem of the temple passed from the realm of the king's private life to that of public affairs.) The building of the temple was a task of major proportions. It required the labor of 183,300 workers. The materials were imported mostly from Lebanon, being supplied by Hiram, king of Tyre, through a treaty with Solomon which gave Tyre, in exchange, great supplies of wheat, oil, and wine. The temple proper was sixty cubits long, twenty cubits wide and thirty cubits high. In the front of the temple was built a porch supported by columns. Many were the materials and decorations needed to make the temple complete. (For details read 1 Kings 6, 7.) The building was begun in the fourth year of Solomon's reign, four hundred and eighty years after the Exodus. It was finished seven years later. In addition to the temple, Solomon also constructed a royal palace (1 Kings 7).

Solomon built a navy at Ezion-geber on the shore of the Red Sea. (1 Kings 9:26). With the help of the seagoing people of Tyre, the navy was manned and brought much wealth into the coffers of Solomon's treasury. Thus, it appears that this was a merchant fleet, rather than a fleet of warships (1 Kings 10:22).

Isaiah. Perhaps the greatest of all the writing prophets was Isaiah. His prophecy is placed first in the books of major prophecy and continues to hold first place in prophetic use by students of Scripture.

Life and Times (Isa. 1-8; 37-39). Not a great deal of the life of Isaiah is known for certain, and most of the material is conjectural; that is, derived from suppositions made from certain hints given in the writings themselves. It is known that he was the son of Amoz, and that he prophesied during the reigns of Uzziah, Jotham, Ahaz, and Hezekiah, kings of Judah. In connection with the history of the kings, Isaiah is mentioned in various passages, particularly in the reign of Hezekiah. When Judah was threatened by Sennacherib, king of Assyria, Hezekiah called for Isaiah who promptly replied that God would deliver them from the menace. Isaiah also was the instrument by which God prolonged the life of King Hezekiah by fifteen years. The Bible shows that he was married and had two sons (Isa. 7:3; 8:3). Tradition holds that at the age of ninety he was placed in the trunk of a tree and sawn asunder, reference undoubtedly being made to this in Heb. 11:37.

Writings (Isa. 1-66). The Book of Isaiah is priceless for more than one reason. Besides being the great book of prophetic utterances that it is, it is considered by the literary experts to be the work of a literary genius. This is the reason Isaiah is such a treasure—it is considered so from both the religious and the literary standpoint. The book contains sixty-six chapters, which compare to the sixty-six books of the Bible. It is the largest of the written prophecies and therefore, is placed first in the order of the Old Testament prophetical books.

Isaiah is known as the "prophet of righteousness," his theme being that God requires righteousness and that sin will be punished (Isa. 1). In Isaiah's prophecy are found both utterances made directly to the people of his own day, and those made with no relation to his own time. It is these latter passages which hold so much interest to the present-day student of Scripture. It must be realized, however, that most prophecy has two applications—one to events contemporary to the prophet, and one to events of the future. Most of the Old Testament Scripture is a "type and shadow of things to come."

One great message of Isaiah to the world is the Messianic message—the predicting of the great King who will rule the world (Isa. 7:14; 9:6, 7). So many statements are made which so definitely apply or fit to the circumstances surrounding the birth and life of Jesus Christ that it is impossible for a spiritually-minded person to deny the inspiration of God. John the Baptist's preaching (Isa. 40:3), the virgin birth of Jesus (Isa. 7:14), rejection of the word by the Jews, the healing power of Jesus, and His shameful death on the cross (Isa. 53) all are brought out in a clear manner by the Prophet Isaiah. Many New Testament passages confirm these prophecies.

The "remnant" message of Isaiah is also an interesting one. This, of course, has Messianic elements, for the remnant has prophetic reference to the followers of Jesus Christ, through whom salvation shall be brought to the world (Rom. 9:27, 28). The substance of the "remnant" prophecy is that, although most of Israel was to be destroyed, a remnant would be saved. This could have several applications, but space does not permit discussion of them here. Suffice it to say that the prophecy has both a natural and a spiritual meaning.

Jeremiah. Jeremiah is the second of the major prophets and is the author both of the book which bears his name, and also of the third of the five books in this group. His authorship of Lamentations is confirmed in 2 Chronicles 35:25.

Personal Facts and Historical Setting (Jer. 1; 26; 32; 36-43). Jeremiah was the son of Hilkiah, a priest. God called Jeremiah while he was yet a child, in the thirteenth year of the reign of King Josiah. He prophesied during the reigns of Josiah, Jehoahaz, Jehoiakim, Jehoiachin, and Zedekiah, kings of Judah. This covered approximately the years from 626 B.C. to 587 B.C. However, his life extended for several years into the period of captivity.[28]

During the reign of Jehoiakim, the nation of Judah made an alliance with the king of Egypt. Jeremiah recognized that the nation rather to be feared was Babylonia (Chaldea), and God gave to Jeremiah a message which foretold the ultimate destruction of Judah at the hands of Nebuchadnezzar, king of Babylon. His assertion that certain doom was impending brought upon him an accusation of treason and he was imprisoned. The taking of his life was prevented only by the plea that the Prophet Micah had made the same prediction years before and had gone unmolested. However, Jeremiah was still forced to undergo persecution because of the message that burned within him and which he could not refuse to preach. Regardless of the constant suffering, he continued to preach that which God had given him. Persecution might destroy the messenger, but the truth of his message was unassailable.

Years later, during the reign of Zedekiah, Nebuchadnezzar besieged, captured, and destroyed the city of Jerusalem according to the words of Jeremiah. Jeremiah was still very much alive, and the Babylonian king gave him the choice to go with the captives to Babylon or to remain with those left behind. He chose to stay and was subsequently carried to Egypt as a prisoner by his own people (Jer. 43:6, 7).

The Jews had fled to Egypt to escape the Chaldeans, but Nebuchadnezzar, in his upsurge of world conquest, assailed the Egyptian kingdom and brought it to his feet. The time of Jeremiah was one of terrific clashes between great Oriental world powers, with the resultant rending of little Judah. It was a very sinful time, the Jews getting further and further away from the God of their fathers. It was because of their sinfulness and their refusal to return to God that their city was destroyed and they were carried captive by the heathen.

Writing (Jer. 1-52; Lam. 1-5). Two books written by Jeremiah are included in this discussion—Jeremiah and Lamentations. They comprise a total of fifty-seven chapters of the most mournful and dark prophecy ever uttered. Jeremiah is constantly lamenting the terrible sin of Judah and the fact that this sin is bringing upon the people the wrath of God. It is a darker picture than that painted by Isaiah, and Jeremiah thereby earns the title of "the weeping prophet." He warned the people that their idolatry was leading them to certain destruction at the hands of the Gentile nations and that great numbers of the Jews would be destroyed. Again, however, the prophecy of the "remnant" makes its appearance as it does in nearly all the prophecies. The dark side has one bright spot—from this terrible destruction a remnant shall be saved from which shall come the Saviour of the world.

This brings up the Messianic prophecies again. As in Isaiah, the prophecy of Jeremiah contains numerous specific references to the Messiah. One passage in the New Testament which specifically states that a certain happening attending the life of Christ was a fulfillment of Jeremiah's prophecy is found in the second chapter of Matthew. It refers to Herod's putting to death all the babies in his province in order to be certain of the death of the one destined to be the Messiah (Jer. 31:15; Matt. 2:18).

Jeremiah prophesied that the Jews would be in captivity for seventy years, at the end of which they would return to restore Jerusalem. Three scriptural references are found in the Old Testament which bear out the fact that this prophecy of Jeremiah was fulfilled when Cyrus, king of Persia, allowed the Jews to return to Palestine. It is mentioned in 2 Chronicles, Ezra, and Daniel.

Several "figures" were used by Jeremiah to teach object lessons, but the one which is the most familiar and with the greatest lesson to us is the "potter and the clay" (Jer. 18:1-11). The vessel was marred in the potter's hand, so he broke the vessel and re-made it according to his will. So is the Lord's power over His creation, and thus it should be with the children of God that they be pliable and easily molded to the will of God. Other figures used by the prophet are the girdle as a type of destruction (13:1-11), the bottles and the wine (13:12-14), and the good and bad figs (ch. 24).

The Lamentations of Jeremiah are a collection of several poems which deal with the great sins of Jerusalem and her sore punishment at the hands of an angry God. But nowhere in it can be found any rancor against God; rather, there is emphasized that the Lord's mercy is great and that His anger is more than justified, due to the terrible sins of the people. Jeremiah has undoubtedly caught the repentant state of the people and their great sorrow over the fall of the city. The captivity, it seems, broke their haughty spirit and made them aware of the power of the great God. However, despite the sorrow of the poet, there is hope that the former glory can be restored, and that all is not dark and hopeless.

Ezekiel. Not a great deal is known concerning the early life of this prophet. His father was a priest named Buzi. Ezekiel lived at approximately the same time as Jeremiah and Daniel. Most of his life was spent in exile, for he was carried captive by the Babylonians in the captivity of Jehoiachin. It must be remembered that before the final destruction of Jerusalem by Nebuchadnezzar, King Jehoiachin had been overcome by the Babylonians and a group of captives taken from Jerusalem. The "great captivity" did not begin, however, until several years later when King Zedekiah was defeated and Jerusalem destroyed. Thus, Ezekiel was a captive long before the major portion of his people were uprooted from their homeland. Most of this writing was done while he was in Chaldea, his home at this time being among the Hebrew captives who were settled on the banks of the River Chebar (Ezek. 1:3). He was probably married and lost his wife due to a sudden and unknown cause. All his utterances predicting the captivity of Jerusalem were prophecies concerning the approaching destruction of Zedekiah's kingdom, and did not refer to events which had already happened.

Prophecy (Ezek. 25-40). Some of the most interesting and comment-arousing things are included in the Book of Ezekiel. It is characterized by some of the most colorful word-illustrations imaginable. It falls naturally into five divisions. The first section covers the first three chapters and is concerned primarily with the call and preparation of the prophet. It contains Ezekiel's vision of the living creatures and the wheels, and his commission from God to preach unto the children of Israel.[29] God's command that he eat the roll of the book is strikingly similar to the command given to John the Revelator in the New Testament. Chapter three contains the divine instruction to the prophet as to his procedure in delivering God's message.

The second division is a long section ending with the twenty-fourth chapter. It is concerned almost entirely with the prophet's gloomy predictions concerning the impending fall of Jerusalem and the great captivity of the nation of Judah. These twenty-one chapters give, in a great wealth of detail, repeated warnings that the evil of the nation is bringing God's wrath to bear upon the city of Jerusalem. By object-lessons, visions, and parables, Ezekiel's message goes forth, despite hostile receptions and disbelieving audiences. The great proof of Ezekiel's divine call and message is that his prophecy was fulfilled to the letter when King Zedekiah's resistance was broken by the combined weight of famine in Jerusalem and the besieging armies of Nebuchadnezzar.

Chapters 25-32, inclusive, recount God's judgments against the nations other than Israel and Judah. They contain many predictions concerning the inevitability of God's vengeance on these nations which had opposed His chosen people. Ezekiel predicted the downfall of nearly all the great cities and kingdoms of the Near East, including the empires of Assyria and Egypt. His prophecies have been literally fulfilled.

The fourth section contains the description of the new Israel, which, in reality, is a prophecy of Christ and His Church. God promises, through the mouth of Ezekiel, that Israel shall be restored, and that God "will give you an heart of flesh." Also in this section is found the famous chapter where Ezekiel preaches to the "dry bones," whose resurrection is a type of the restoration of Israel and the coming of the kingdom of God.

The last nine chapters of the book give minute details concerning the restoration of Israel and God's plans for setting up the temple. The dimensions and details of a new temple are given; particulars of the restored priesthood and the various religious ordinances are presented. This appears to be the plan upon which the temple of Zerubbabel was based and after which the restored government was modeled.

In addition to these divisions there are some general points of interest. Ezekiel was a man who used a great many object-lessons to get his point across. One example of these is the use of the prophet's hair to typify the destruction of Israel (Ezek. 5). God told him to shave his head and to divide the hair into three equal parts. The first third he burnt in the fire; the second third he cut in pieces with a knife; and the last portion he scattered in the wind. The burnt hair represented that a third of the Jews would die by pestilence; the hair cut with a knife typified that another third of them would perish by the sword; the scattered hair was a sign that the rest would be scattered over the face of the earth. But God instructed Ezekiel to take from the number a few strands of hair and save them, which represented the Word of the Lord, "Yet will I leave a remnant." Other object-lessons and parables too numerous to mention in detail are the siege (Ezek. 4); foreshadowing of Zedekiah's captivity (Ezek. 12); parable of the eagles and the vine (Ezek. 17); the boiling pot (Ezek. 24).

Another element in Ezekiel's prophecy, which differs quite a bit from Isaiah and Jeremiah, is the great number of visions it contains. Each of the other prophets saw visions at times, but Ezekiel it seems received most of his messages through these divinely inspired visions. These were awe-inspiring and endowed the prophet with great boldness to preach the messages they contained, to those people for whom they were intended.[30] Some of these are very familiar. The vision of the wheels (Ezek. 10) and the vision of the valley of dry bones (Ezek. 37) have been made very well-known through both sermon and song.

As in the other prophecies previously studied, Ezekiel also has its share of Messianic predictions. One of importance is the statement that in the future there will be one flock, one shepherd from the house of David, and that a new covenant will be established (Ezek. 34:20-31). Ezekiel, it seems, stressed the value of following the Spirit of the Lord rather than being bound to the letter of the Mosaic law (Ezek. 36:25-27).

Nehemiah. Almost an hundred years after the first return, Nehemiah, the king's cupbearer and a Jewish captive, entreated King Artaxerxes to commission him to return to Jerusalem to rebuild the walls of the city which had never been repaired since they had been broken down by Nebuchadnezzar over one hundred fifty years before. Permission was granted, and Nehemiah returned to Jerusalem as governor to begin immediately the task of repairing the wall.[31] Despite vigorous opposition by Tobias and Sanballat, the wall was finished in the amazingly short time of fifty-two days. Helping him in this endeavor was Ezra, who had returned from captivity a few years before Nehemiah.

Daniel. Daniel is the last of the major prophets. His work is small in size when compared to the other prophecies, but the importance of the book lies not in its length, but in its content.

Relation to World History (Dan. 1; 5; 6; 10). Nothing is known of Daniel's family. His first introduction to history is his being carried into Babylon in the captivity of Jehoiachin, mentioned in the life of Ezekiel. Once in Babylon, Daniel, together with three other Hebrew youths, was taken into the service of the royal court and each was given a new name.[32] It was here that Daniel and the others refused to eat the king's meat or drink his wine with the result that they were healthier by far than the ones who had partaken.

Three years later, Daniel was called upon to interpret the dreams of King Nebuchadnezzar. This he did, by the power of God, and as a reward he was made one of the chief men of the Babylonian empire. The first of Nebuchadnezzar's dreams was of the great image made of various materials, which was destroyed by the stone hewed out of the mountain. This will be discussed later. Eventually, however, Nebuchadnezzar died and other kings arose who kept Daniel in the background. During the reign of Belshazzar he received a vision which revealed to him the future of the great nations and empires which were then in existence and those which were yet to rise. This is the vision of the four great beasts and kingdom of God (Dan. 7).

It was during the reign of Belshazzar that Daniel interpreted the handwriting on the wall which had thrown the king's banquet into confusion. The interpretation that the kingdom would fall into the hands of the Medes and Persians was not long in fulfillment, for that very night the invading armies were at the gates of the city and Belshazzar was slain. Darius, the new king, appointed Daniel the "third ruler of the kingdom." This high position aroused the jealousy of his enemies who persuaded the king to pass a decree designed to stop Daniel from praying. Daniel didn't stop, and, as a result, he was thrown into the den of lions, from which God miraculously delivered him.

Daniel's death is not recorded. No fact can be found which clearly establishes the date and circumstances of his death, so the student is in total darkness on that score. However, it is fairly certain that he died in Babylon. The time of his life was the period of the great captivity of Judah, but he lived to see the fulfillment of Jeremiah's prophecy that the Jews would return in seventy years.

Prophecy (Dan. 1-6; 7-12). Daniel's prophecy, it seems, falls into two natural parts. The first six chapters relate Daniel's life in the court and his relationship with the various kings that occupied the throne. It is written in the third person, relating events as though the writer were not a part of the action. Too, there is not one account of a vision which was seen by Daniel himself. The second six chapters deal entirely with the visions of Daniel and show no direct association between Daniel and the kings, although they are mentioned. It is this last part which has really earned for the book its position among the books of prophecy.

The prophecy is only twelve chapters long, but its effect is tremendous. No other writing so vividly and accurately foresees the rise and fall of the great kingdoms of the world as Daniel's account of the king's dream of the great image (Dan. 2). The head of fine gold, breast and arms of silver, belly and thighs of brass, legs of iron, and the feet of iron and clay mixed together represent, respectively, the empires of Babylonia, Persia, Greece, and Rome. The stone which destroyed the image represents Christ and His kingdom which would remain after all other kingdoms had fallen.

As has been mentioned, Daniel also received his great messages through visions. God, it seems, dealt with him in a special way, revealing to him the secrets of the ages. Most of the visions are contained in the last few chapters and all of them are Messianic. Daniel even uses the word "Messiah" in the famous prophecy of the seventy weeks. Daniel's Messianic prophecies, it seems, draw comparisons between the temporary existence of earthly kingdoms and the eternal duration of the kingdom of Christ.

Scholars for years have pointed out the great similarities in style and content between the books of Daniel and Revelation. Both of them are concerned with happenings in the last days. Both of them relate great visions while the writer is carried away by the Spirit of the Lord. Too, it seems there is perfect harmony and agreement between the two. This letter, of course, helps further to clinch the belief in the inspired nature of the Bible.

Objective: The individual will demonstrate an understanding of the content of the Old Testament by describing the significance of the following events: the call of Abraham, the Exodus from Egypt, the establishment of the covenant at Sinai, the institution of the Levitical sacrifices, the conquest of Canaan, the rule by judges, the establishment of the monarchy, the division of the kingdom, the exile in Babylon, the return from captivity.

Bible Training Institute, General Bible Study: *pp. 43-45*
Bible Training Institute, Lessons in Bible Training,
Vol. I , pp. 15-58

The Call of Abraham. In this period we see the transition from God dealing with the entire human race to the choosing of a certain family through whom to perform His will. This does not mean that henceforth He never again spoke to anyone or bestowed blessings and favors upon anyone but Abraham and his seed (notice Job, for instance). But it does mean that to a special family was entrusted the knowledge of God, His laws, His will, and His plan of salvation. That family was Abraham and his descendants.

Faith (Gen. 12; 15; 22). Abraham's whole life was one of faith. By faith he was able to stand the test and receive the promise. Yet, he himself did not receive the fulfillment of that promise (Heb. 11:13). Abraham's dispensation was one of faith and preceded the dispensation of law.

Melchisedec (Gen. 14). Melchisedec's place in prophecy is enlightened by the writer of Hebrews, who compares him with Christ (Heb. 7:1-22).

Hagar and Sarah (Gen. 16; 21). The allegory of the freewoman and the bondwoman is plainly interpreted by the writer of Galatians (4:21-31). This contrasts grace and legality and gives a spiritual application to the story of these two women which is not borne out by the natural events, for Sarah's descendants later received the law.

The Exodus From Egypt. This is one of the most important periods in the history of the Jewish people (and of the worship of the true God). In this era the family of Israel becomes the nation of Israel approximately two million strong. Also in this period, the people of God entered the dispensation of law, which continued for hundreds of years until the coming of Christ. The following spiritual lessons can be drawn from events of this period.

The Passover (Exod. 12). This event in the history of the Jews is of great importance to us. The lamb sacrificed at this time is

———————————

Bible Training Institute, op. cit.

typical of Christ, the Passover Lamb of God sacrificed for the sins of the world. The blood sprinkled on the doorposts is typical of the blood which covers our sins. The death of Egypt's firstborn (representing the wicked) tells us that without blood there is no remission of sin, while the salvation of Israel's firstborn is typical of the salvation of the righteous whose sins are under the blood.

The Law (Exod. 20). A study of the law and its many lessons for us would, in itself, comprise a large volume, so we may take only a fleeting glance at it. Why was the law given? It was given that sin might be made manifest and easily recognizable (Rom. 3:20; 7:12, 13); it was given as a shadow of good things to come and as a schoolmaster to bring us to Christ (Gal. 3:24, 25). God promised to write the law upon the hearts of the people that the commandments might be kept (Jer. 31:31-34), a promise which was fulfilled in Christ.

The Brazen Serpent (Num. 21). This was a type of Christ, for the New Testament expressly tells us: "And as Moses lifted up the serpent in the wilderness, even so must the Son of man be lifted up: That whosoever believeth in him should not perish, but have eternal life" (John 3:14, 15). This serpent appears again from time to time in the history of the Jewish nation, in most instances an object of idolatrous worship, until it was destroyed by Hezekiah, king of Judah (2 Kings 18:4).

The Establishment of the Covenant at Sinai. This lesson is in the same chronological period as the wandering in the wilderness, but the emphasis is on the Law of Moses rather than a Jewish history. The children of Israel went into Egypt a family numbering seventy persons; they came out of Egypt a nation of approximately two million people. This new nation of Israel was a theocracy. Every phase of their life was tied up inextricably with religion. God was the head of the state—all decisions of any importance were handed down by Him. He worked through individuals, however, since the time of direct administration was past. The center of Jewish life of this period was the tabernacle. The human agencies of rule, judgment, and discipline were the priests. Sins or crimes were considered as such against God rather than against the state or individuals as they are now considered. The lesson has been divided up according to the emphasis of the various laws, but since laws of religion were the basis for all other laws, political or social, it will be well to keep this in mind as the lesson progresses.

The Decalogue, or Ten Commandments, forms the most important section of the whole law, for it provides the foundation upon which all other laws are based, and it sets the standard for the moral and ethical life of the people. However, it must be recognized that the people were incapable of keeping the commandments to the fullest extent, and that very few of them succeeded in making even a fair bid toward complete observance of God's laws. Then, if the law as based upon the Ten Commandments could not be kept, why was it given? The apostle Paul answered it well as he said, "Wherefore the law is holy, and the commandment holy, and just, and good. Was then that which is good made death unto me? God forbid. But sin, that it might appear sin, working death in me by that which is good; that sin by the commandment might become exceeding sinful" (Rom. 7:12, 13). Therefore, we can see that the law was given that sin might be made manifest and easily recognizable. However, we as Christians know that the law was merely a shadow of good things to come (Heb. 10:1), and that God had promised to write the law upon the hearts of people that they might be able to keep the commandments of the Lord (Jer. 31:31-34). This promise was fulfilled with Christ.

The Institution of the Levitical Sacrifices. *Religious and Ceremonial Law.* Jewish ritual and ceremony were very elaborate and involved. They were burdensome and difficult to comprehend fully. There were offerings and sacrifices for every contingency and every situation, with each sacrifice accompanied by its own elaborate set of symbols and ritualistic devices. There were good reasons for this, however. We have learned that the law was given because of transgression and not to prevent transgression, for the law was incapable of preventing it. The New Testament writers have given us a preponderance of evidence that Christ must needs die (Acts 17:3) because the law could not accomplish the salvation of men. But until that time there was a necessity for some plan whereby man and God might meet in reconciliation. This necessity was met by the law, which was indispensable, in that it kept men aware of God's eternal presence and power, at the same time that it pointed out and foreshadowed the grace dispensation to be ushered in by Christ.

The Conquest of Canaan. This period of history saw a promise fulfilled. The land of promise became the land of possession as the new nation of Israel actually subdued its population. This was a period of unity and close cooperation of the tribes. They were held together by pressure of necessity plus the statesmanship and religious fervor of Joshua. However, though the Israelites gained ascendancy over most of the heathen peoples, they did not completely subdue them and destroy their identity. This failure, in turn, caused Israel to espouse their idolatry in time.

The following are some spiritual lessons which can be drawn from a study of this period:

Joshua, a Type of Christ (Josh. 1:1-9). To begin with, the names Joshua and Jesus are the same, both meaning "savior." As Joshua was a savior of his people, so is Christ our spiritual Saviour. As Joshua led Israel into the land of milk and honey, so Christ leads God's children into the spiritual promised land. Joshua was the leader of the second phase of Israel's redemption, that is, possession. Christ is our redemption.

Possession and Conflict (Josh. 3-5). It is interesting to note that the wars and conflict did not end with the entering of Canaan. To most of us, possession of Canaan represents complete victory, but this is not true so far as the Christian life is concerned. Although a sanctified person has victory over sin, we must still do battle against the forces of Satan. However, the final outcome is sure—we shall be victorious.

Rahab's Faith (Josh. 6). Rahab was the woman who befriended the spies in Jericho and thereby saved herself and her house from death. The writer to the Hebrews tells us that by faith she escaped the destruction that fell upon the unbelievers. Even though she had been a wicked woman, by believing, she received salvation. By faith she believed, escaping death; by faith she believed and became the ancestress of Jesus Christ (Matt. 1:5). James also tells of her works, for true faith brings works which are then accepted as righteousness. (Heb. 11:31; James 2:25). Notice in the story, also, that she was saved through the use of a red cord which represents the shedding of blood without which there is no remission of sins (Heb. 9:22). Rahab is one more instance where the value of the Old Testament in our day is proven.

The Rule by Judges. The events of our lesson reflect the character of the times. The people of Israel were under a theocratic government (rule by God), and this was the only unity they knew. Although the people of the twelve tribes were related by blood, language, history, and religion, they were politically divided along tribal lines. During this period there was no central authority except the priesthood, and at times open war broke out between tribes. They were surrounded by hostile and warlike peoples who constantly harassed them. As long as they were true to the worship of God, they were unified and victorious; but once that fellowship with God was broken, they fell easy prey to their enemies and to their own internal weaknesses. The times are also pictured in Judges 17:6: "In those days there was no king in Israel, but every man did that which was right in his own eyes."

Here are some specific examples of spiritual lessons to be gained from events in this Old Testament period:

Gideon at Work (Judg. 6-8). The Lord seldom, if ever, calls a lazy man to work for Him. Paul, for instance, was hard at work against the cause, but he began to work just as hard for it. If we can only serve the Lord as we would serve ourselves, then He will be pleased with our efforts.

Jephthah's Rash Vow (Judg. 11). This passage can open to us several things to consider concerning vows to God. (1) Be careful what you vow, for (2) you will be responsible for keeping it; however, be diligent in performing your vows, for in so doing (3) you will be blessed (Ecclesiastes 5:4, 5).

The Establishment of the Monarchy. This period saw a transition from a loosely knit group of twelve tribes into a united and strong Israel under three able kings. This one hundred twenty years is the "mountaintop" of Israel's existence. However, beneath the surface the divisive forces were still at work and would break forth with the first great crisis. The people of God were still under the dispensation of law, although the kingdom had turned the government from a theocracy to a monarchy.

The Davidic Covenant (2 Sam. 7). One of the great spiritual truths to be gained from a study of this period is the covenant by which the throne of David was to be established forever. This is, of course, prophetic of Christ and His kingdom. Jesus was "made of the seed of David according to the flesh" (Rom. 1:3); therefore, this prophecy has a literal and spiritual fulfillment.

David and the Temple (1 Chron. 22). It is interesting to note, too, that David was not allowed to build the temple, for he was a man of war. Several things can be seen from this: God's house is a house of peace; there is great merit in making preparations for another man's work in order to further it; David's zeal in the task is a wonderful example; and his lack of ill will, because his most cherished dream was denied him, is also good to follow.

The Division of the Kingdom. The persons of this period are so numerous that it is impossible to settle upon a few to characterize. In general, the character of the northern kings was evil, their hearts continually filled with idolatry and self-will. There were some able leaders among them, but their downfall was religious and moral failure. The character of the southern kings was mixed. There were some exceptionally fine characters such as Hezekiah and Josiah, but there were extremely wicked ones as well. At the last, the inner wickedness of the people prevailed, resulting in their captivity. In striking contrast to the mixed characters of the kings, the prophets of the period stand out as beacons of righteousness and as spokesmen for the God of Israel.

The period was one of "ups and downs." Divisions replaced unity, although the divisive forces had always been lurking beneath the surface. It became a time of judgment, in which God visited upon them the inevitable results of their disobedience. God is long-suffering, but He will not withhold the scourge forever.

The Prophets (2 Chron. 20:20; 24:19; 36a;16). Throughout the study of the great events of this period, frequent mention has been made concerning a group of men known as the prophets. These men were spokesmen for God, crying out against personal and national wickedness. They were raised up as witnesses against their generation, for God always warns, leaving no excuse when punishment is meted out. Many of these prophecies were given specifically for their day and serve us only as examples. Others hold twofold (or even more) meaning: one for their day, and another for ours; a natural or outward meaning, and a spiritual meaning.

Seven Thousand True Worshippers (1 Kings 19:18). "Yet I have left me seven thousand in Israel, all the knees which have not bowed unto Baal, and every mouth which hath not kissed him" was God's answer to Elijah, who bemoaned the fact that he stood alone in serving God. We need never fear that we stand alone, for God will have a people who will not "bow unto Baal" and who will stand for the right.

Wrong Advice (1 Kings 12). A common failing among people today is their tendency to choose the wrong counsel. The Old Testament story of Rehoboam and his choice of advisers is another of those examples for our benefit. In most cases, the advice of those older in the way of the Lord is more valuable because it is based on a wealth of experience. The rash counsel of youthful inexperience is to be avoided.

Understanding the Vision (2 Chron. 26:5). It was said of Zechariah, the prophet, that he "had understanding in the visions of God." It is not always enough to be a visionary, but it is vital to have understanding as well. The Scripture says, "They have a zeal of God, but not according to knowledge" (Rom. 10:2). In thus referring to the Jews, the apostle Paul meant that they had a vision of the overall program of God, but lacked the understanding of it in relation to them and Christ. Let us seek to have "understanding in the visions."

The Exile in Babylon. This period was one of disaster to the Jewish nation. From the fall of Jerusalem the Jews have had only provincial status under the control of some foreign power. Their masters changed from time to time, and their degree of freedom went from one extreme to another, but always they paid tribute to some foreign government. Too, the great dispersion of Jews first had its beginning at this time, for hereafter, Jews could be found in great numbers in many cities of the ancient world.

The religion also underwent a transformation, for what we know as Judaism really began under the captivity. By Judaism we mean the religion of the Jews so strictly bound up in a rabbinical tradition, interpretations of the law by various scribes, the rise of sects such as the Pharisees, the institution of the synagogue, and the gradual acceptance of the idea that God could be worshiped anywhere—not only in Jerusalem.

The Return. (*Ezra, Nehemiah*). The two Old Testament books dealing with the return to Jerusalem tell of several groups returning at various times. In the first year that Cyrus reigned, a group under Zerubbabel returned and began rebuilding the temple. They numbered around fifty thousand persons. Events of note in the ensuing period: Enemies attempted to stop the building of the temple, Haggai and Zechariah encouraged the work, the temple was completed, and Ezra led another group of returning Israelites to Jerusalem.

The first two returning groups were concerned with the temple and its services. However, the wall of the city was still broken down and stayed thus until the third group returned. This small company of men was led by Nehemiah and had a vital interest in rebuilding the wall. Despite the vigorous opposition of Tobias and Sanballat, the wall was finished in only fifty-two days "for the people had a mind to work" (Neh. 4:6).

Objective: The individual will demonstrate an understanding of the content of the Old Testament by naming the Ten Commandments.

Holy Bible, Exodus 20:1-17

And God spake all these words, saying,

I am the Lord thy God, which have brought thee out of the land of Egypt, out of the house of bondage.

Thou shalt have no other gods before me.

Thou shalt not make unto thee any graven image, or any likeness of any thing that is in heaven above, or that is in the earth beneath, or that is in the water under the earth:

Thou shalt not bow down thyself to them, nor serve them: for I the Lord thy God am a jealous God, visiting the iniquity of the fathers upon the children unto the third and fourth generation of them that hate me;

And shewing mercy unto thousands of them that love me, and keep my commandments.

Thou shalt not take the name of the Lord thy God in vain; for the Lord will not hold him guiltless that taketh his name in vain.

Remember the Sabbath day, to keep it holy.

Six days shalt thou labour, and do all thy work:

But the seventh day is the Sabbath of the Lord thy God: in it thou shalt not do any work, thou, nor thy son, nor thy daughter, thy manservant, nor thy maidservant, nor thy cattle, nor thy stranger that is within thy gates:

For in six days the Lord made heaven and earth, the sea, and all that in them is, and rested the seventh day: wherefore the Lord blessed the Sabbath day, and hallowed it.

Honour thy father and thy mother: that thy days may be long upon the land which the Lord thy God giveth thee.

Thou shalt not kill.

Thou shalt not commit adultery.

Thou shalt not steal.

Thou shalt not bear false witness against thy neighbour.

Thou shalt not covet thy neighbour's house, thou shalt not covet thy neighbour's wife, nor his manservant, nor his maidservant, nor his ox, nor his ass, nor any thing that is thy neighbour's.

The Content of the New Testament

Unit Five

Objectives:

The individual will demonstrate an understanding of the *content* of the New Testament by:

- identifying the theme, and where appropriate, the key events and people of each book of the New Testament.
- describing the life and significance of the following people: John the Baptist, Jesus, Paul, Peter, John the Apostle, James (the brother of Jesus).
- describing the significance of the following events: the Birth of Christ, the Crucifixion and Resurrection, the Day of Pentecost, the Correspondence of the apostle Paul.
- constructing a chronological outline of the main events in the life of Christ.
- tracing on a map the missionary journeys of the apostle Paul.
- naming the Beatitudes.

Resource Guide for Learning Goals and Objectives

UNIT FIVE: THE CONTENT OF THE NEW TESTAMENT

Objective: The individual will demonstrate an understanding of the content of the New Testament by identifying the theme, and where appropriate, the key events and people of each book of the New Testament.

Raymond M. Pruitt, Fundamentals of the Faith, *pp. 18, 19*

The New Testament's twenty-seven books are divided into the following sections:

Biographical (4 books)

Matthew—The Gospel of Christ the King, Son of David (1:1)
Mark—The Gospel of Christ the Servant of the Lord (10:45)
Luke—The Gospel of Christ the Son of Man (19:10)
John—The Gospel of Christ the Son of God (20:31)

History (1 book)

Acts—The History of the Early Church (1:8)

Pauline Epistles (13 books)

Romans—The Gospel of Christ (1:16, 17)
1 Corinthians—The Standard for Christian Conduct (15:58)
2 Corinthians—The Vindication and Conduct of the
    Ministry (5:20)
Galatians—The Law and the Gospel of Grace (1:6-9)
Ephesians—The Unity of the Church (4:4-6)
Philippians—The Joy of Knowing Christ (1:21)
Colossians—The Preeminence of Christ (1:15-19)
1 Thessalonians—The Model Church (1:7-10)
2 Thessalonians—The Second Coming of Christ (2:2)
1 Timothy—The Standard for Church Order (3:14-16)
2 Timothy—Paul, A Good Soldier of Jesus Christ (4:6-8)
Titus—The Order of God's House (1:5)
Philemon—Christian Brotherhood Exemplified (vv. 15-18)

General Epistles (8 books)

Hebrews—The Superiority of the Son of God (7:24-26)
James—Practical Christian Faith (2:18)
1 Peter—Victory Over Suffering (1:6-9)
2 Peter—Christian Growth (3:17, 18)
1 John—The Father's Love Letter to His Children (4:7-10)
2 John—Walking in Truth and Love (v. 6)

Raymond M. Pruitt, *op. cit.,* pp. 18, 19.

3 John—Christian Hospitality Toward Those Who Walk in
    Truth (5-8)
Jude—Contending for the Faith (v. 3)

Prophetical (1 book)

Revelation—The Return of Christ and the Establishment of
His Kingdom (1:18, 19)

Objective: The individual will demonstrate an understanding
of the content of the New Testament by describing the life
and significance of the following people: John the Baptist, Jesus,
Paul, Peter, John the Apostle, James (the brother of Jesus).

Bible Training Institute, General Bible Study, pp. 114-180

John the Baptist. The greatest figure between Malachi
and Christ was the preacher-prophet of the wilderness
known as John the Baptist. In the period of our lesson study
he is the leading figure, for Christ had not been manifested
as yet to the world.

Birth and Life (Luke 1:5-25, 57-80). The birth and parentage
of John is given in the first chapter of Luke, who, it seems
had the historian's knack of recording a wealth of detail. John
the Baptist was born to a priest named Zacharias and his wife,
Elisabeth, earlier in the same year that Christ was born in
Bethlehem. The birth of John was miraculously foretold by the
Angel Gabriel, who appeared to Zacharias as he ministered in
the temple. He announced to the awed priest that to his aged
wife a son was to be born who was "to make ready a people
prepared for the Lord" (Luke 1:17). The awe-stricken
Zacharias expressed his natural doubts as to the probability
of Elisabeth's giving birth to a child at her age, whereupon he
was stricken dumb for his unbelief. His wife became with
child, but his inability to speak remained with him. Six
months later the familiar visit of this same Angel Gabriel to
the Virgin Mary occurred, immediately after which Mary visited
Elisabeth, her cousin, remaining with her three months.
During this time the two women talked together, rejoicing
greatly over the fact that God had singled them out to bestow
upon them this special favor.

Bible Training Institute, *General Bible Study* (Cleveland, TN:
White Wing Publishing House, 1976) pp. 114-180. Used by permission.

Just before the birth of John, Mary returned to Nazareth. When John was circumcised, the cousins and neighbors named him Zacharias, but Elisabeth firmly refused, calling him John. Zacharias, still unable to speak, wrote upon the writing table that his name was John. Immediately his speech was restored, the whole series of events arousing a great commotion over the entire area.

Little else is known of the early life of John the Baptist with the exception of one verse which says that he lived in the deserts "till the day of his shewing unto Israel" (Luke 1:80).

Ministry (Matt. 3:1-12). John the Baptist grew up in the wild hill region of Judea and presented to his audiences probably one of the wildest appearances imaginable. He lived like a recluse in the deserts, clothed in his very modest raiment of camel's hair and eating an even more modest diet of locusts and wild honey (Matt. 3:4). While his appearance was very rough, he attracted great audiences by his passionate, eloquent preaching, and by the fact that here, among the dead and dying precepts of formal religion, a new and vital force was at work—that here was a new living message which promised to shed light in the midst of great darkness.

Location and Duration (Luke 3:1-20). John began preaching in the fifteenth year of Tiberius Caesar, A. D. 25, almost two years before the beginning of the public ministry of Christ (Luke 3:1). His messages attracted great audiences from "Jerusalem, and all Judea, and all the region round about Jordan" (Matt. 3:5). John did not go into the synagogues of the cities, but stayed out in the open country where the people flocked in multitudes to hear and be baptized. He preached to these huge crowds up until his imprisonment by Herod, which occurred not long after the baptizing of Jesus. (Evidence that John continued to preach after Jesus began His ministry is found in John 3:22, 23.) However, from the time that Jesus came up out of the water of the Jordan, John voluntarily gave place to Him as the chosen One of God. He continued to preach, but the writers of the Gospels indicate that his popularity immediately began to wane. His preaching ended, of course, when he was imprisoned, although some of his disciples remained loyal to him.

Message (Mark 1:1-4). "John did baptize in the wilderness, and preach the baptism of repentance for the remission of sins" (Mark 1:4). This, in a nutshell, was the message of John.

The Spirit moved upon him to urge the people to repent, "for the kingdom of heaven is at hand" (Matt. 3:2). He did *not* preach baptism as a means of cleansing from sins; he did *not* baptize those who came to him still unrepentant. He baptized in water,[33] but he preached the "baptism of repentance" for the cleansing of the people's sins. When John saw people coming to be baptized whom he knew were not sincere, he refused to baptize them until they brought "forth therefore fruits meet for repentance" (Matt. 3:8). This was a new message in that it did not recognize the efficacy of sacrificial offering for the "remission of sins." The Scripture says, "The law and the prophets were until John: since that time the kingdom of God is preached" (Luke 16:16). No longer were people bound by the fetters of the law and sacrifice, but had access by repentance to the kingdom of God. This was John's message.

In addition to his message of repentance, John declared the divine nature and purpose of Jesus Christ whom he confessed to be the Messiah and the only begotten Son of the Father (John 1:15-18).

His Position in Relation to the Messiah (Mark 1:5-8; 6:14-29). "The voice of him that crieth in the wilderness, Prepare ye the way of the Lord, make straight in the desert a highway for our God" (Isa. 40:3). This is the prophecy of Isaiah concerning one who was to go before the Messiah, preparing the way. This same prophecy is that quoted by John the Baptist when he denies the suggestion that he is the Christ or one of the prophets. Too, his claim that he was the forerunner of the Christ is seen to be included as part of his preaching, for he was determined that none of the people should be deceived concerning his identity. Over and over he tells the people that there is coming one after him who is to be a figure of far greater power than he. In addition to the Prophet Isaiah, the book of Malachi also makes reference to the "messenger" who was to prepare the way (Mal. 3:1). This preparation took the form of the doctrine of repentance, which is the groundwork upon which a Christian life is based.[34] John, in his preaching, stated that he was baptizing with water (which we have shown to be subsequent to and as a witness of repentance), but that there was one coming after him who would baptize with the Holy Ghost and fire. John continually prepared the way for Christ by pointing out the kingdom of God and that repentance was the key for opening the door. Too, by his quick and complete acceptance of Jesus as the Christ he convinced many in his huge audiences that it was true. Many are the ways in which John the Baptist prepared the way for the public ministry of Christ, fulfilling his part on the program of prophecy.

Jesus. Very little of Jesus' life from His birth to the beginning of His public ministry is recorded in the four Gospels. However, from the time of His baptizing in the River Jordan, the accounts suddenly become full of His activities and His teachings. The first four books of the New Testament are biographies of His life, but, in reality, the only portion of His life which is dealt with in any but a sketchy fashion is the last three years. It was in these last three years that He was made manifest and that His great teachings were given to the world. The early years of His life were not unimportant, but were relatively insignificant when compared to the great events and significance of the last three years. The writers of the New Testament were impressed with the necessity of brevity. Books were all written by hand and were made into very bulky scrolls. In consequence of this, ancient writers were very careful to condense their writings as much as possible and to leave out everything that was not absolutely necessary. The writers of the New Testament biographies of Jesus were very responsive to the inspiration of God and felt that God Himself was directing them in the choice of material for their books. We know that the things that remain unrecorded in their books would make a much larger book than all four of their accounts combined. John himself says, "And there are also many other things which Jesus did, the which, if they should be written every one, I suppose that even the world itself could not contain the books that should be written" (John 21:25).

It is impossible to cover all the ground in the New Testament accounts of Jesus' life. Therefore, it is necessary that we choose only a few of the most important or of the most interesting points of the story. These will merely be high spots, which will point out the supposed chronological sequence of events.

Preparation and Time of Obscurity. Immediately after Jesus was baptized of John in Jordan, the Spirit led Him into the wilderness to be tempted of the devil. This temptation was Christ's final preparation before He began to fulfill His mission upon earth. The first several months, which approximate one year, were spent in apparent obscurity. He did not attract the great crowds which followed Him at a later period, mainly because He did not work the great miracles which were characteristic of His subsequent ministry. Also, He was quietly gathering those disciples, later known as apostles, who were to be with Him throughout the years ahead and who were to be the great leaders in the spread of Christianity over the face of the earth after His death. Too, the ministry of this first year was merely a continuation of the work of John the Baptist. Jesus baptized, through His disciples, and preached repentance and the kingdom of God, the same message preached by John the Baptist. Many people were baptized and heard His preaching, but still the great press of huge throngs did not begin until later on.

The Temptation (Matt. 4:1-11). After Jesus was baptized, and after God had acknowledged Him as His Son in such a marvelous way, the Spirit led Him into the wilderness. Here Jesus fasted for forty days and forty nights, which, since His divine spirit was residing in a fleshly temple, produced in Him a great physical hunger. At the time when Jesus was physically the weakest, Satan began buffeting Him with the temptations. These temptations were not after the manner of those which beset carnal man, who is "drawn away of his own lust, and enticed" (James 1:14), but they were designed to cause Jesus to make a premature display of His divine power at the suggestion of Satan himself. Success in this plan would have brought to nought the plan of God. However, this eventuality is inconceivable. The first temptation was to command that stones be made bread, to which Jesus answered, "Man shall not live by bread alone but by every word that proceedeth out of the mouth of God" (v. 7). This was an appeal to gratify the appetite, to give in to the natural desires of the flesh, to make use of His divine power to satisfy His own hunger. Then the devil tried to persuade Him to make a spectacular leap from the pinnacle of the temple, which Jesus answered by quoting, "Thou shalt not tempt the Lord thy God." This was a very sly suggestion that the way to win popularity, the way to show His identity to the multitudes, was to perform something spectacular in a rather fruitless fashion. The third temptation was the offer of the kingdoms of the world in return for the Son of God's falling down to worship the evil one himself. Again Jesus quoted the Old Testament: "Thou shalt worship the Lord thy God, and him only shalt thou serve" (v. 10). This last and greatest temptation was to give in to the Jews' conception of the kingdom of God, to show His great power in a worldly way, setting up a world empire with Jerusalem at its center. But none of these "temptations" moved our Lord. He defeated every attempt of the devil to persuade Him to yield to his suggestions. The devil gave up trying, left Jesus, and the angels ministered unto Him. (This temptation is also recorded in Mark 1:12, 13 and Luke 4:1-13.)

The First Miracle (John 2:1-11). The only record of the remainder of the first year of Jesus' ministry is found in John, the others making only bare references to it. John tells of Jesus attending the marriage feast in Cana at which His mother was also present. When the wine ran out, Jesus told the servants to fill the waterpots with water. After they had done this, they were told to take from the pots and serve. Miraculously the water had become wine; in fact, the best wine at the feast. "This beginning of miracles did Jesus in Cana of Galilee, and manifested forth his glory; and his disciples believed on him" (John 2:11).

Meeting With Nicodemus (John 3:1-15). Following this first miracle, Jesus, with a group of disciples, went down to Jerusalem after having spent a few days in the Galilean city of Capernaum.[35] The reason for His visit at this time was to observe the Passover. On this visit the first cleansing of the temple took place, and He performed quite a few miracles in the city (John 2:12-23).[36] These miracles brought to Jesus the first Jewish ruler, who came at night to inquire about the marvelous things that Jesus was doing. Then Jesus laid down to Nicodemus, and to us, the simple requirements for entering the kingdom of God. "Except a man be born again, he cannot see the kingdom of God" (3:3). This, of course, is no physical rebirth, since, as Nicodemus says, a man cannot be born of his mother a second time. It is a spiritual birth, by which a man is born into the kingdom of God.[37]

The Samaritan Woman (John 4:1-30). After talking with Nicodemus, Jesus began preaching and baptizing in the region of Judea, this continuing for quite some time. Then He left Judea and journeyed north, passing through Samaria on the way. He stopped at a well to refresh Himself and engaged in conversation with a woman of the region. This is the first indication that Christ was come to minister to any people who were not purely Jewish. He told the woman many things concerning herself, amazing her that He knew the very thoughts of her heart. Then, to her, He announced His

106

Messiahship! Immediately she began to spread the news, and many people of the region believed on Him. During His interview with this woman, He taught her the essence of true religion. The Samaritans worshiped in the mountain, the Jews worshiped in the temple at Jerusalem, but Jesus informed her that "the hour cometh, and now is, when the true worshippers shall worship the Father in spirit and in truth: for the Father seeketh such to worship him. God is a Spirit: and they that worship him must worship him in spirit and in truth" (John 4:23, 24). Jesus remained with the new Samaritan believers for two days and then journeyed on to Galilee.

Time of Popular Favor. After performing the second miracle in Cana—He healed the nobleman's son, who was in Capernaum—Jesus left Galilee to return to Jerusalem to attend a "feast of the Jews" which evidently was the Passover. Immediately He aroused the ire of the "Jews"—which John calls them, but who were evidently the Pharisees and Sadducees mentioned by other writers—who sought to kill Him because He healed on the Sabbath and claimed to be the Son of God. The sermon that Jesus preached showed the relationship between the Father and the Son and soundly rebuked the Jews for manifesting such a spirit (John 5). From Jerusalem He returned to Galilee where He entered what we shall call the time of popular favor. It was a period when He performed many of His greatest miracles, and attracted to Him His greatest crowds of admirers and followers. This period is sometimes called the Galilean ministry for it was, in the main, spent in that region with His headquarters at Capernaum.

Sermon on the Mount (Matt. 6-8). Probably the greatest sermon that has ever been preached was delivered by Jesus Christ early in the second year of His public ministry. After praying all night, Jesus called His disciples to Him and of them chose twelve whom He named apostles. (The names of the twelve are found in Matt. 10:2-4; Mark 3:13-19; and Luke 6:13-16.) After this meeting with the twelve, He began preaching to the people who were gathered around Him. His words were primarily addressed toward His disciples, but the whole multitude heard Him. This message includes the famous "Beatitudes" (Matt. 5:1-12) and many other teachings whose value to the Christian cannot be reckoned. But explicitly Christ states in this sermon His relationship to the law and prophets, and the differences between the kingdom of God and the traditions of the Jews. His teachings on murder, adultery, swearing, and various other points in the Jewish customs were so much stronger and were given such a new and righteous emphasis as to comprise a compete new set of guides of conduct. The Sermon on the Mount contains instructions for nearly every phase of the Christian life, and any life modeled after the pattern set forth therein will measure up to God's standard of righteousness. The people stood and listened to Him, astonished at His doctrine, "for he taught them as one having authority, and not as the scribes" (Matt. 7:29).

Healing of the Woman With an Issue of Blood (Mark 5:22-34). Many things took place between the Sermon on the Mount and this great act of faith on the part of the woman and the manifestation of the healing virtue of the Son of God. He taught and preached in many cities of the region of Galilee, performing healings and miracles as He went. In Gergesa, across the Sea of Galilee from the province of Galilee, He healed the man who had a legion of devils, permitting them to enter a herd of swine nearby, which immediately plunged over a cliff, destroying the entire herd in the sea. After this occurrence He returned to Capernaum, where this famous miracle took place. He was on His way to the house of Jairus, whose daughter was very sick. As always, He was surrounded by a clamoring, insistent mob, beseeching Him to satisfy their desires. In this crowd was a woman who had spent all her savings to the doctors in an effort to find a cure for an "issue of blood." Fearing that she could never get the notice of the Master in such a crowd, she felt that if she could only touch Him unawares, she would receive the long-sought-for healing. She struggled with all her puny might, and by some great effort she reached out her hand and barely brushed the hem of Jesus' robe with her fingers. Instantly she was healed, another testimony of the miraculous combination of human faith and divine power. Jesus astonished His disciples by asking who had touched Him, for He was being jostled on every side, but He knew that great faith had been exercised, since He had felt "virtue" flow out of Him. When He saw to whom the healing power had gone, He said to her, "Daughter, thy faith hath made thee whole" (Mark 5:34).

Time of Opposition. Jesus continued to preach, to work, and to administer to the ills of the people for He "was moved with compassion on them" (Matt. 9:36). Besides this, He gave His disciples power to work miracles and sent them out to preach to the "lost sheep of the house of Israel" (10:6). He gave them many instructions concerning their relationship with their Master and foretold many things which would be theirs to suffer for the cause of Christ. This marks the beginning or near the beginning of His third year before the public. From this time He began declining in public favor, especially after preaching the sermon on the bread of life in the synagogue at Capernaum (John 6:26-71). Jesus had been preaching, teaching, traveling, and performing miracles for a little over two years. In that time He had gathered a handful of faithful followers, a huge throng who followed Him for the benefits they might receive, and had stirred the bitter animosity of the prejudiced and hide-bound Hebrew sects, which even now were seeking ways to kill either Him or His influence. John the Baptist had been imprisoned and beheaded as the price he had to pay for preaching the gospel. Now Jesus was entering on the last full year of His ministry before He, too, must pay the supreme price, only with greater significance and meaning to the world.

Feeding the 5,000 (Mark 6:30-44).[38] The multitudes had followed Jesus out to the desert places so that they might be healed, and as the day was far spent, Jesus' disciples besought Him to send them away to procure food for themselves. Jesus amazed His disciples who undoubtedly thought He was jesting when He told them to feed them. They protested the scarcity of food—five loaves and two fishes—but He took this little lunch, blessed it, and gave it to His disciples to distribute to the multitude. When everyone had eaten, they gathered up the fragments which filled twelve baskets—all from five loaves and two fishes. How could anyone deny His power after such a miracle wrought at His hands?

Divinity of Jesus (Matt. 16:13-20). While on the way to Caesarea Philippi, Jesus talked with His disciples and asked them a few questions, probably some of the most important questions which were ever pointed toward His disciples. If you will recall the Jewish conception of the coming of the Messiah, you will immediately see the significance of the questions that He asks. The Jews had hoped to see a great warrior Messiah who would come, destroy their enemies by His might, and set up a great world rule, with the Jews in the seat of power. They expected Him to come with great manifestation of military and political power—they did not expect Him to be born in a lowly stable; they did not expect His kingdom to be a spiritual one. Therefore, when Christ asked the question, "Whom do men say that I, the Son of man, am?" and the answer was, "Some say that thou art John the Baptist; some, Elias; and others, Jeremiah, or one of the prophets," it can be seen that the Jews had not then, nor ever have for that matter, accepted Jesus as the Messiah. But then Jesus asked, "Whom say ye that I am?" Peter's answer, as spokesman for the twelve, was: "Thou art the Christ, the Son of the living God." Such a declaration could have come not from "flesh and blood"—for the Jews (and Peter was a typical Jew) were prone to judge by the flesh—but from God. Thus, on the rock of Peter's revelation of the divinity of Jesus Christ did Christ say He would build His church, "and the gates of hell shall not prevail against it" (v. 18).

Transfiguration (Matt. 17:1-13). From the time that Jesus declared His purpose to build the church, He began teaching His disciples how He must suffer and die. Six days afterward, Jesus took His disciples up into a high mountain to pray;[39] and as He prayed, Jesus was transfigured before them, His clothing becoming glistening white. Two men, Elijah and Moses, appeared with Jesus, discussing the great sacrifice of Jesus which was to take place in Jerusalem. Peter, and the two with him, had fallen asleep before this miraculous and glorious vision appeared. As they awoke from their sleep and beheld the vision, the ever-rash Peter blurted out, "Lord, it is good for us to be here: if thou wilt, let us make here three tabernacles; one for thee; and one for Moses, and one for Elias" (v. 4). The sudden sight of this heavenly scene had so dazzled and frightened Peter that he did not know what to say. Then a cloud suddenly shrouded the three figures of Jesus, Moses, and Elias, and out of the cloud came a voice saying, "This is my beloved Son. . . hear ye him" (v. 5). The cloud lifted as suddenly as it came, leaving Jesus alone with His three disciples. He enjoined them that they should keep what they had seen to themselves until He should be risen from the dead.

Ten Lepers (Luke 17: 11-19). On the way from Galilee to Jerusalem Jesus came into a certain village where He met ten lepers who stood off from Him and beseeched Him to have mercy on them. Jesus, always compassionate, told them to go show themselves unto the priests—which was a part of Jewish law (Lev. 13)—and as they went, they were all healed. But one of them, a Samaritan, when he saw that he was healed, ran back to Jesus and fell upon his face at His feet, pouring out his gratitude. Jesus asked him, "Were there not ten cleansed? but where are the nine? There are not found that returned to give glory to God, save this stranger."[40]

Lazarus Raised From Death (John 11). Shortly after Jesus entered the last four months of His life, word reached Him in Bethabara, where He had been staying, that their friend Lazarus, the brother of Mary and Martha, was sick in Bethany, near Jerusalem. Jesus did not go immediately, but waited for two days, until Lazarus died. This He did "for the glory of God" (v. 4), and that His disciples might believe. He took His disciples; and when they arrived in Bethany, they found that Lazarus had been dead already for four days. Amid all the lamenting and regrets of the dead man's sisters, acquaintances, and friends they went to the cave where the body of Lazarus was entombed. Jesus, to the amazement of all, asked for the stone which sealed the entrance to be rolled away. Then He commanded, "Lazarus, come forth" (v. 43), and he came, bound hand and foot in the customary grave clothes. "Loose him, and let him go" (v. 44), said the Lord, and great numbers of the amazed crowd that witnessed it believed on Him. This miracle, and the subsequent conversion of these people, just added fuel to the flames of hatred which were already burning in the hearts of the chief priests and Pharisees. This miracle was a foretaste and foreshadowing of the even greater power which was to bring Christ from His grave on resurrection morning.

Beginning of Passion Week. Early in the last week, the events of the coming days began to shape up. Jesus arrived on the outskirts of Jerusalem on the first day of the week.

The Triumphant Entry (John 12:12-19). Jesus sent two of His disciples into a certain village where they were to find an ass and her colt, which they were to bring to Him. When they had done so, they placed their garments on them, making a place for Jesus to sit. In this manner Jesus entered the city of Jerusalem and as He rode, the great crowd which had gathered spread their clothing in the street and cut branches to place in the road, all the while crying, "Hosanna to the son of David: Blessed is he that cometh in the name of the Lord; Hosanna in the highest" (Matt. 21:9). It seemed to be a moment of great triumph, and no doubt the disciples felt that the moment had come when the Messiah would manifest Himself and assert His power. His entrance had moved the whole city, and it probably seemed as if the time to set up His kingdom had arrived. Jesus rode on to the temple, where, for the second time in His life, He chased out the moneychangers and rebuked these people for making of God's house a "den of thieves" (Matt. 21:13). Afterward, He healed many that came to Him in the temple. But He didn't display any great power and returned quietly to Bethany to spend the night.

Predictions Concerning Death (Mark 10:32-34). Before they had ever arrived in Jerusalem, Jesus had talked to His disciples concerning His approaching death and resurrection. He told them specifically that He would be betrayed into the hands of Jewish leaders who would condemn Him, deliver Him to the Gentiles to crucify Him, and that on the third day He would rise again. However, it seems as though the disciples still did not understand that soon their Lord would be taken from them and put to a shameful death. Yet all during the fore part of the week of His crucifixion, He continued to make pointed remarks which indicated that His death was near. He gave them many instructions which would apply only to the time when He was no longer with them. When Mary anointed His feet with the oil, He said of her, "She is come aforehand to anoint my body to the burying" (Mark 14:8). Other hints of His coming humiliation are too numerous to mention (John 12:23-36).

Other Events (Mark 13). The triumphal entry took place on Sunday, the first day of the week. On the following Tuesday, Jesus went as He had done before, to the temple to teach and to heal. But this time He was met by a deputation of Jews who attempted to entrap Him with fatal arguments so that He might be accused of blasphemy. He turned their own questions upon their heads and held them up to just ridicule before the listening throngs. After this He went to Mount Olivet, where He taught concerning the events of the "last day." The next day was probably when Judas Iscariot interviewed the chief priests concerning his desire to betray Jesus into their hands.[41] On Thursday He sent Peter and John into the city to make preparations for the observance of the Passover.

Upper Room and the Garden. On Thursday evening the Lord and His disciples, including Judas, met in an upper room of the city, to observe the Passover supper together. This was to be their last meeting before Jesus was hailed before the Sanhedrin and condemned to death as a blasphemer.

Important things took place in this meeting—occurrences which have influenced nearly all the subsequent history of mankind. Notice, first, the manner in which the place for the supper was chosen. Peter and John were sent with the instructions to follow a man carrying a pitcher of water (Mark 14:13). Where he stopped they were to ask the proprietor of that house the whereabouts of the guest chamber where the Master may eat the passover with His disciples. This they did and had everything ready when the time came.

Lord's Supper and Feet-washing (Matt. 26:17-30; John 13:1-17). As soon as they had seated themselves to eat, the Lord began telling them that one of the number would betray Him. In alarm, they began to inquire which one it might be. Jesus showed that it was Judas, but somehow the disciples still did not understand who it should be. During the supper, He took bread, gave thanks, broke it, and gave it to His disciples. He told them that this bread was His "body which is given for you," and instructed them to continue to do this "in remembrance of me." In the same manner, He instructed them concerning the cup which they shared after supper, telling them that the wine "is the new testament in my blood, which is shed for you" (Luke 22:19, 20). Thus, Christ instituted the universally-recognized ordinance of the Lord's Supper, or communion. But Christ also inaugurated another just as sacred and just as important an ordinance, which, strange as it may seem, has never been accepted by most of the churches of the world. This was the observance of feet-washing. The Scripture says, "He riseth from supper, and laid aside his garments; and took a towel, and girded himself. After that he poureth water into a basin, and began to wash the disciples' feet, and to wipe them with the towel wherewith he was girded" (John 13:4, 5). This gives in detail the procedure which Jesus followed. Peter objected greatly when it came his turn for the Lord to wash his feet. Jesus rebuked him by saying, "If I wash thee not, thou hast no part with me," whereupon Peter, in his characteristic impetuous way, said, "Lord, not my feet only, but also my hands and my head." After the Lord had completed His round of all the disciples with the basin and towel, He told them, with just as strong an admonition as He had used in connection with the supper, "If I then, your Lord and Master, have washed your feet; ye also ought to wash one another's feet" (John 13:14).

The Traitor (John 13:18-30). The name of Judas Iscariot has lived in infamy since the day on which he betrayed the

Son of God. The bargain with the priests probably had been made on Tuesday evening (Luke 22:3-6) and the events in the upper room took place on the evening of the following Thursday. After Jesus had all but pointed His finger at Judas and shouted, "There is the traitor," the account in John indicates that Satan took complete possession of Judas, and he went out to carry out the evil bargain which he had made.[42]

The Garden (Matt. 26:36-56). After the supper and after they had sung a hymn (or psalm) Jesus took His disciples across the brook Kidron to the Garden of Gethsemane at the foot of the Mount of Olives. Then He took Peter, James, and John, going a little farther to pray. The great burden of the coming sacrifice was now weighing heavily upon Jesus. It was natural that His flesh rebel at the thought of dying in the very prime of life, Jesus being only about thirty-three years old. He knelt in the garden to pray that God would allow the cup of death to pass Him by. That prayer, accompanied by such untold agony of spirit and body, is known by all Christian people everywhere. Despite the desire of His body to live, Christ was willing to do the will of the Father, even though He knew it meant cruel mockery and death on the cross, which at that time was a symbol of the most shameful death which could be inflicted as a public sentence. So He prayed, "not my will, but thine, be done" (Luke 22:42).

After He had prayed and had been wonderfully strengthened for the ordeal ahead, He and His disciples were still in the garden when Judas, the traitor, arrived with the throng of priests and temple guards to deliver Christ into their hands. After the betrayal kiss, the armed men gathered around Jesus to take Him, whereupon the impetuous Peter drew his sword and cut off an ear of the high priest's servant. Christ rebuked Peter and restored the man's ear. The temple delegation then took Jesus and delivered Him to the Sanhedrin to be tried before them, Jesus' disciples fleeing in fright.

Paul. *Conversion of Saul* (Acts 9:1-31). While not occurring in Samaria, this significant event did take place about the time that Samaria was being evangelized. The gospel had spread as far north as Damascus, the capital of Syria, and Saul got permission to go to the synagogue of that city to bind and return to Jerusalem any that he found there who had believed on the name of Jesus. He was not very far from his destination when suddenly a great light shone about him, causing him to fall to the ground. He heard a voice saying, "Saul, Saul, why persecutest thou me?" (v. 4). While he lay there on the ground, Saul was instructed to go on into the city where he would be further instructed. Saul's eyes were blinded, but his men led him by the hand the rest of the way. After he waited for three days in his blind condition, the Lord spoke again, this time to Ananias, telling him to go to the street called Straight where he would find Saul. Knowing the reputation of Saul, Ananias was reluctant to go, but God told him that Saul was a chosen vessel and to have no fear. Ananias did as he was bid, and through him Saul was released from his blindness and received the Holy Ghost. From that day Saul began preaching the very name which he had persecuted before with such boundless vigor. Although he was mistrusted at first by the brethren, it was not long until Paul was befriended by Barnabas, who paved the way for more intimate relations with the Church.

Ministry of Paul (Acts 12-28). Immediately after the events in Damascus, Saul, better known as Paul, began preaching the gospel in the synagogues. Fairly soon afterward he was sent by the brethren to his home in Tarsus. Not much is known concerning his stay there, which evidently lasted several years.

Life and Background (Acts 22:3-21; 26:1-23). Saul was a Jew born in Tarsus, a Roman city in Asia Minor in the district of Cilicia. (See map of Paul's first missionary journey.) He was well-educated, probably knowing several languages—at least Greek and Hebrew. He was a Roman citizen (22:25-30), probably inherited from his father. Although he was born in Tarsus, he evidently spent most of his early life in Jerusalem studying under the famous Pharisee rabbi, Gamaliel (22:3). He, himself, was, until his conversion to Christianity, a strict Jew of the sect of the Pharisees (26:5). At the time of the martyrdom of Stephen he was still a young man pursuing his studies in the capital of Judaism. However, all his time was not spent in studying the law, for all Jewish boys had to learn a trade. His trade was tentmaking, which he probably used to good advantage many times in financing his missionary journeys (18:1-3).

Missionary Journeys (Acts 13; 14; 15:36-21:17). Paul was called of God to minister unto the Gentiles (9:15, 16). To that end most of his life was dedicated. After Paul had been in

Tarsus for some time, word reached the Church at Jerusalem of a great evangelization of certain regions of Asia Minor. They sent Barnabas to go as far as Antioch, but he first went in search of Paul.[43] Together they went to Antioch where they worked and preached for a whole year. At the end of that year the church there was directed by the Holy Ghost to send Barnabas and Paul to preach to the Gentiles.

The First Journey (Acts 13; 14). While it is impossible to point out every detail in every stage of their journeys in the space allotted, a few more important occasions can be mentioned. On this first trip Paul was accompanied by both Barnabas and John Mark. The entire mission was spent in an area not too far removed from Antioch. Paul's method was to go directly to the synagogue in each city and preach the Word to those gathered to worship there, a goodly number of whom were Gentile proselytes, mostly Greeks who had been attracted by the religion of the Jews.

On the island of Cyprus in the city of Paphos, Paul was called by the deputy of the island, a man named Sergius Paulus, who desired to hear the Word preached. With this man was a certain Jewish sorcerer named Elymas who resisted Paul in his efforts to convince the Roman of the truth of the gospel. Paul, being led by the Holy Ghost, rebuked the false prophet, pronouncing upon him the judgment of God that he would lose the sight of his eyes for a season. Immediately his sight left him, necessitating someone to lead him around by the hand. The ruler, when he had witnessed the power of God, believed in the doctrine taught by Paul.

When they left the island of Cyprus, they went to Pisidian Antioch, where Paul preached a very wonderful sermon in the synagogue there, recounting for his hearers some of the history of the Israelites and showing how this tied in with the coming and death of Jesus Christ. Many believed, and the jealous Jews stirred up so much persecution against them that it was necessary for them to leave.

In the course of events they came to Lystra, a city in the region of Lycaonia. Paul, through the power of God, healed a crippled man who had been practically helpless from birth. When the people of the city saw this miracle, they thought that the "gods" had come to visit them. The pagan priest and the people of the city prepared to do sacrifice upon them, believing them to be Jupiter and Mercury come to earth. Paul, with difficulty, constrained the people from doing such, explaining that they were only men preaching the gospel of the living God. Not long after this, the two men returned to Antioch (Syria), and the first journey was over.[44]

In order that the student may follow the journey easily on the map, here is the order in which the various places were visited on the first journey: Seleucia; Cyprus (Salamis, Paphos); Pamphylia (Perga); Pisidia (Antioch); Iconium; Lycaonia (Lystra, Derbe); Pisidia; Pamphylia; Attalia; and return to Syrian Antioch.

Council at Jerusalem (Acts 15). When Paul and Barnabas returned to Antioch, a group of men came there from Jerusalem teaching the people that they could not be saved unless they practiced circumcision as taught under the law. These two missionaries rebuked the doctrine, feeling that such a requirement was unnecessary. The question raised such a disturbance that Paul and Barnabas, along with some others, were sent by the church at Antioch to confer with the apostles and elders at Jerusalem. After some discussion in which Peter, Paul, and Barnabas took part—all of those feeling that circumcision was not necessary—James, the moderator of the assembly, spoke his advice on the matter. He asked that the Gentiles be freed from such a binding restriction and that the assembly unanimously agree to this. The Church unanimously consented to the proposal, so letters were dispatched by chosen men to the churches of the Gentiles so that they might be informed of the decision.

Second Journey (Acts 15:36–18:22). After the council at Jerusalem, Paul returned to Antioch, where he made preparations to take another trip. He and Barnabas separated over a difference of opinion on whether to take John Mark along with them. Paul would not consent to it, so Silas accompanied him instead. Along the way, Luke evidently joined them, for the author begins to include himself in the narrative (16:11).

After preaching and establishing churches in various regions of Asia Minor, the missionaries stopped off in Troas, a coastal city on the Aegean Sea. It was there that Paul received the vision of the man of Macedonia, begging him to "come over into Macedonia, and help us" (v. 9). Knowing that this was a divine message, they immediately made plans to ship over to that Greek territory. They eventually made their way to Philippi, the chief city of the region.

In Philippi there was a young girl who had a "spirit of divination" who, by her ability to predict the future, brought to her masters quite a bit of money. This girl encountered Paul's party and began following them around in the streets, crying, "These men are the servants of the most high God, which shew unto us the way of salvation" (v. 17). This she did for several days, until one day Paul rebuked the spirit which possessed her and restored her to her right mind. Her masters, realizing that their source of profit was gone, were very angry and hailed Paul and Silas before the magistrates, charging them, as Jews, with having taught things contrary to Roman law. They were beaten and thrown into jail. But at midnight Paul and Silas were praying and singing when suddenly a violent earthquake shook the prison, opening all the doors and loosening all the shackles. The shock awakened the keeper, who, seeing the prison wide open, was going to kill himself with his sword when Paul cried out, "Do thyself no harm: for we are all here" (v. 28). The keeper, recognizing in these mysterious events the hand of God, began to beseech them to tell him how he could be saved. In the dead of night, Paul and Silas preached to the jailer and his household, all of whom believed and were baptized. In the morning the magistrates, having heard that the prisoners were Roman citizens, came down to the prison in a very repentant mood to release the prisoners.

After leaving Macedonia, Paul visited in Greece proper, coming eventually to Athens itself. When Paul beheld the way in which the city was completely absorbed in idolatry, he was stirred. His preaching aroused the curiosity of the philosophers who took Paul to the Areopagus to inquire about the "new doctrine." Paul then stood in their midst, telling them about "the unknown God." He preached them a sermon in which he exhorted them against the worship of idols. He told them that they must repent and mentioned the resurrection of Christ, whereupon they mocked him, not believing in the resurrection. A few of the men and women believed what he had said before he took his leave from the city. He visited in Corinth and then began his journey back to Antioch where the second journey was ended.

The following is the order in which the various places were visited on Paul's second journey: Syria; Cilicia; Derbe and Lystra; Phrygia; Galatia; Mysia; Troas; Macedonia (Samothracia, Neapolis, Philippi); Amphipolis: Apollonia; Thessalonica; Berea; Athens; Corinth; Ephesus; Caesarea; and back to Antioch.

Third Journey (Acts 18:23-21:17). Paul did not stay in Antioch long. Soon he was on his way to the churches of the

Gentiles. After traveling in Galatia and Phrygia, he arrived at Ephesus where he stayed for three years. There he found a few people who were disciples of John the Baptist who had never heard of the Holy Ghost. He taught them and they, too, received the baptism of the Holy Ghost. But probably the most important happening was the trouble with Demetrius the silversmith. Paul's preaching had turned many people away from idolatry who heretofore had bought from the silversmiths many small shrines, which was their chief source of income. This loss of income angered the silversmiths, who were led by Demetrius in arousing the city's animosity against Paul and the others. The city was in an uproar for hours, the confusion and disorder getting almost out of hand. However, the town clerk finally managed to quiet the demonstration of the worshipers of Diana and defended the Christians as being peaceful and law-abiding men. He warned the people that such an uproar would have to be accounted for to the governor and that, if there were any charges to be made against these men, it would be done in lawful assembly. Then he dismissed the mob.

After this near-riot, Paul went into Macedonia and Greece for quite some time. He then retraced his route on the way back to Jerusalem. When he arrived in Miletus, feeling that he did not have time to visit Ephesus, he sent for the elders of the Ephesian church to come to Miletus that he might speak to them. He reviewed for them the work he had done in their midst and exhorted them to continue in the faith, warning them of troubled waters ahead for the flock. Enjoining them to beware of some of their very number who would rise up and draw away disciples from the church, he let them know that this would probably be the last time they would ever see him. After he had finished his message to them, he left the sorrowing group and boarded ship for the remainder of his trip to Jerusalem.

The following traces the route of the third journey: Galatia; Phrygia; Ephesus; Macedonia; Greece (probably as far as Corinth); Philippi; Troas; Assos; Mitylene; Chios; Samos; Miletus; Coos (or Cos); Rhodes; Patara; Tyre; Ptolemais; Caesarea; Jerusalem.

Trip to Rome (Acts 21:26–28:31). Although Paul had been warned in Caesarea that he would be bound in Jerusalem and be delivered to the Gentiles, he was determined to go. After he arrived in Jerusalem, it was not long until he had been taken by the Jews and accused of teaching against the law of Moses and of profaning the temple by bringing Greeks within the sacred enclosure. Of course, the charges were false or misleading, but these Jews from Asia were determined to put him down. He made a noble defense before his Jewish audience, telling them of the miraculous nature of his conversion, but it only angered them the more. They turned him over to the Roman soldiers for trial, but he pleaded his Roman citizenship. So the Roman captain called a council of the Jews to inquire into the matter. In this meeting Paul caused the Jews to argue among themselves by bringing up the controversial subject of the Resurrection, on which the Pharisees and Sadducees were divided. Paul was taken from this meeting, after which forty Jews made a solemn vow neither to eat nor drink till Paul had been killed. Learning of their intent, the Roman soldiers escorted Paul to Felix, the Roman governor. He remained in prison under this man's care for about two years. In the course of events, Paul's appeal to Caesar made it necessary for him to be sent to Rome, but space does not allow us to mention these events in detail.

Following is a brief outline of the events which took place on Paul's last journey—the trip to Rome. Taking a ship from Caesarea, Paul and company came eventually to "The Fair Havens" in Crete. When they sailed from there, they were shipwrecked on the island of Melita (Malta) where the incident with the poisonous serpent and the healing of the chief's father took place (28:1-11). Getting another ship, in due time they arrived in Rome. Once in Rome Paul was allowed quite a bit of liberty, living in his own rented house for two years, preaching to all that came to hear him, without incurring any governmental opposition. The exact date of Paul's martyrdom is not known for sure, but as far as we know, he never left Rome alive.

Two of the seven General Epistles were written by the apostle Peter, probably during the later years of his life. These come, in the New Testament arrangement, immediately following the epistle of James. The letters were both written with the same audience in mind, although not at the same time.

Later Life (Acts 2-5; 9:32-12:19; Gal. 2:1-16). It is rather pointless to go into a lengthy discussion of the early life of Peter, either as a fisherman of Galilee or one of the chosen twelve. This portion of Peter's life has been touched upon in the lessons on the life of Jesus and in the study of the Early

Church. However, a short review might be helpful. We meet him first as a fisherman called to be a fisher of men. All during the life of Jesus he occupies a very prominent place among the twelve, not merely through an arbitrary choice of Christ, but because of his characteristics which naturally fitted him to be a leader among them. After his denial of Christ we find him repenting bitterly and later being reinstated to his position among the twelve. And during the years of the Early Church Peter is much in evidence. He instituted the proceedings in the upper room by which Matthias was chosen to succeed Judas to make the circle complete. He was present when the Holy Ghost fell, and we hear him delivering his bold message on the new Christian religion to the amazed multitudes. Later we see him healing the impotent man at the gate of the temple, being led of God to deliver the message to Cornelius, preaching the word in Samaria, suffering beatings and imprisonment for the sake of the gospel.

Much later, during the ministry of Paul, he appears again in the history of the Acts in connection with the question arising over the circumcision of Gentile converts to Christianity, in which Peter was somewhat at fault for siding with the party of the circumcision through fear of their influence.[45] However, Peter reasserted his courage, and at the decisive meeting in Jerusalem, championed the cause of the Gentiles. From all this we gather that one of the most important personages of Early Church history was the apostle Peter.

Probably his ministry was mostly confined to Palestine and its outlying districts. Very little of Peter's later life is known for a certainty, but several strong traditions have come down to us, which at least are not at variance with Scripture. It is believed that Peter did visit Rome in the last year of his life and suffered martyrdom at about the same time as Paul.[46] Paul and Peter were great friends (2 Pet. 3:15) even after the controversy over circumcision, for, in view of Peter's espousing Paul's cause at the council at Jerusalem, it appears that Peter realized that Paul had been right in rebuking him for slighting the Gentiles. Undoubtedly the rebuke had been administered in a spirit of humility and love, not with haughtiness and ill-temper. Peter was in all probability crucified (Jesus had apparently predicted that in John 21:18, 19), and the tradition which holds that he requested to be crucified upside down because he was not worthy to die in the same manner as Christ is in keeping with what we know of Peter's character.

John wrote three epistles in addition to the other books to his credit (Gospel of John and Revelation). These three epistles are among the latest to be written of the books of the New Testament. They were written quite a few years after all the rest of the original twelve apostles were dead.

Biographical Sketch (Matt. 4:18-22; Mark 3:17; 10:35-45; John 19:25-27; 21:1-25; Acts 3:1-11; 4:13-22; 8:14; Gal. 2:9). As in Peter's case, we are already acquainted with John, the "beloved" apostle. However, since it seems he does not stand out as much as Peter, a little more detailed review might prove helpful. John was one of the sons of Zebedee, a fisherman on the Sea of Galilee, probably not of the poorer class, however. At first, John was a disciple of John the Baptist, but left him to follow Jesus after John had pointed Him out as the "Lamb of God." He was chosen by Christ to be one of the twelve apostles, and he, together with his brother James, received the surname Boanerges (sons of thunder). John was the only apostle to witness the crucifixion of the Son of God, and at the cross Jesus appointed him to care for His mother.

After the death of the Lord, Peter and John appear as very close friends. They worked together, preached together, suffered together. Fifteen years after Paul's first visit, John was still in Jerusalem, was one of the leaders of the Church, and participated in the apostolic council in Jerusalem, at which was made the settlement of the controversy between the Jewish and Gentile Christians (Acts 15:6, 13; Gal. 2:9).

History gives very little data concerning the later life of John. All that we know for certain is that he spent most of the later years of his life at Ephesus and at one time was exiled on the isle of Patmos. In addition to this, as in the case of Peter, many traditions have come down across the years. One of the most famous of these is the story of his being boiled in oil during one of the severe Roman persecutions, escaping with no harm since God would not allow him to be killed. We are certain that he lived to an extreme old age, outliving all the other apostles and was the only one of the twelve to die a natural death. Near the end of his life it appeared that he was much too feeble even to get about from place to place, so he was carried by the brethren to the place of worship.

John, as an apostle, was very close to the Lord, being one of the three leading disciples and was called, in addition, the disciple "whom Jesus loved" (John 13:23). John's settling in Ephesus probably occurred after the death of Mary. John was courageous, physically strong, but having a kind, lovable nature.

James. This book is placed first among the seven General Epistles. The reasons for this are not known, but it is one of the largest of the books, and bears the name of the first pastor of the headquarters' church in Jerusalem. The epistle of James was probably written before the council in Jerusalem, possibly before A.D. 49. At any rate, it was written quite some time before Paul's epistles.

Biographical Sketch (Matt. 13:55; Acts 15:12-21; 21:18-25; Gal. 2:9). The author of this epistle is generally agreed, except by some modern critical scholars, to have been James, the brother of Jesus. It is easy to become confused when one speaks of James, for there were quite a few prominent men in the Early Church who bore this name. However, it is fairly certain that the author of the letter was the brother of the Lord. Many modern—and sincere—critics believe that he was really only the cousin of Jesus, identifying him with one of the twelve listed as "James, the son of Alphaeus" (Matt. 10:3). Alphaeus is known to have been the husband of Mary's sister—whose name was also Mary—thus making this James the cousin of the Lord. However, this opinion is held primarily by those who insist upon the perpetual virginity of the mother of Jesus, a view for which there is no scriptural foundation. There is absolutely no reason to believe that Mary did not live a very normal life after the birth of Jesus, and that, as any other Jewish woman, had several other children during her lifetime. The size of her family was not very large due to the relatively early death of Joseph, who was evidently quite a few years older than Mary. So, it is fairly certain that James of the twelve (10:3) and the author of this epistle (13:55) were two different men.

The passage in Matthew 13:55 and Mark 6:3 point out that James, together with several brothers and sisters, were the children of Joseph and Mary. Evidently Jesus' brother did not believe in Jesus at first (John 7:5), and continued in his disbelief until after the Resurrection, for the first record we have of James being among the believers is the upper room (Acts 1:13, 14). Yet the rise of James to prominence in the Early Church was rapid. In him was recognized some of the qualities of leadership possessed by Jesus, which, added now to his intense devotion to the cause, made of him a valuable man to the Church. In a very few years James had so proved his value as to have been chosen as pastor of the church in Jerusalem. At the assembly in Jerusalem he is recognized by the delegates as the moderator of the gathering, and, as can be clearly seen by his authority in the matter under discussion, must have been considered a prominent leader in the Early Church.

Of his later life we know very little. An Early Church historian mentions that James was killed by the Jews, who threw him from the pinnacle of the temple and beat out what life remained in him with a fuller's club. At any rate, it is fairly well established that he died a martyr's death as a result of upholding the faith.

———————

Objective: The individual will demonstrate an understanding of the content of the New Testament by describing the significance of the following events: the Birth of Christ, the Crucifixion and Resurrection, the Day of Pentecost, the Correspondence of Apostle Paul.

Bible Training Institute, General Bible Study, *pp. 118-159*

The Birth of Christ. *Early Life of Jesus* (Matt. 1; Luke 2:39-52). "Behold, a virgin shall conceive, and bear a son, and shall call his name Immanuel" (Isaiah 7:14). These are the words of the Prophet Isaiah uttered over seven hundred years before the birth of Christ, which is undoubtedly the prophecy which was fulfilled when Jesus was born of the Virgin Mary in a stable of Bethlehem of Judea. Mary was the espoused wife of Joseph, a man of the tribe of Judah and lineage of David. Their home was Nazareth, but at Jesus' birth they had traveled to Bethlehem in response to a decree by Augustus Caesar that all the world should be numbered and taxed, each person in his own city. Since Bethlehem was the city of David, it was necessary for Joseph to journey there to obey the decree. Thus it was that the emperor of Rome

———————

Bible Training Institute, *General Bible Study* (Cleveland, TN: White Wing Publishing House, 1976) pp. 118-159. Used by permission.

helped to fulfill the prophecy that Jesus was to be born in Bethlehem of Judea (Mic. 5:2).

Birth and Genealogy (Matt.1; 2; Luke 1:26-56; 2:1-40; 3:23-38). Probably the world's best-known story is that of the birth of Jesus, the visits of the shepherds and wise men, and the flight of the family into Egypt. However, it is worthwhile to point out a few less-obvious facts concerning this glorious time. The shepherd's visit took place on the very night that Jesus was born, and nearly all accounts of the happenings surrounding His birth leave the impression that the wise men came at about the same time. However, this could not have been true. The wise men came from a great distance in the east and evidently had been following the star for quite some time. Also, by the time they arrived, Jesus had been removed from the manger and was found by them in a house. (The account of the visit by the wise men is recorded only in Matt. 2:1-12.) Most chronological tables show the visit of the wise men occurring at least a month or two later than that of the shepherds, certainly not until after He had been taken to the temple to present Him to the Lord. (The shepherd's visit is recorded in Luke 2:1-20.)

The lineage of Joseph has been mentioned in connection with the census. Matthew begins his book by tracing from Abraham down to Joseph the entire genealogy of Jesus Christ. In summing it up, he states that there were fourteen generations between Abraham and David, fourteen between David and the captivity in Babylon, and fourteen from that time till Christ's birth in Bethlehem about 4 B.C. However, in the third chapter of Luke, the line of Christ is traced all the way back to Adam, taking a little different line. Evidently, Luke's list takes one side of the family while Matthew follows the other. Both of them use the same genealogy between David and Abraham.

The Crucifixion and Resurrection. *Trial and Crucifixion* (Matt. 26:47-27:56). While the disciples had been together in the upper room, Jesus had hinted very strongly concerning His imminent death. He singled out Simon Peter to tell him that the happenings of this night would cause him, as well as the others, to fail in the test. Peter had protested that he would never forsake the cause. Jesus then told him that before the cock crew, Peter would deny Him three times. This prediction became a reality as Peter stood outside in the court while Jesus was being tried before the Sanhedrin.[47]

The Sanhedrin (Matt. 26:57-75). Jesus was first taken before Annas, the former high priest, who still retained the title by virtue of his age and influence. Annas then sent Jesus to Caiaphas, the current high priest and leader of the Sanhedrin (John 18:13). Sometime in the early morning—one or two o'clock—Jesus was tried informally before certain members of the supreme Jewish council. It was during this time that Peter's denial took place. At dawn, the Sanhedrin met officially and delivered a verdict of death for the crime of blasphemy. However, since a sentence of death had to have official Roman approval, it was necessary for them to take Jesus before Pontius Pilate, the Roman officer in charge.

Pilate (Luke 23:1-25; John 19:1-16). Pontius Pilate was very reluctant to confirm the sentence passed by the Jewish council. He felt that Jesus was not guilty of any wrongdoing, and, therefore, not deserving of such severe punishment. However, several things caused him to give in to the Jews' demands. Pilate's record in Palestine was not a particularly bright one. So, when the Jews let Pilate know that they would, in all probability, raise a cry to Caesar if he freed Jesus, it caused Pilate to reconsider his good intentions. Too, he thought that by showing his reluctance and by going through the ceremony of washing his hands of the whole affair, it would absolve him of all guilt. Probably other motives entered into his decision to permit the Jews to carry out their plans. Pilate, before he gave in completely, thought that there was one chance for the Jews to change their minds. It was the Roman custom to release one popular prisoner to the people every Passover. So, in mentioning this to the people, Pilate probably thought that Jesus' former popularity with the mass of the people would cause them to ask for Jesus' release. But instead—the "leaven of the scribes and Pharisees" had been at work—the mob cried, "Release unto us Barabbas," and "crucify" Jesus (Luke 23:18, 21).

After Pilate delivered Jesus to the Roman soldiers, these tough Roman legionnaires began to have a little amusement at Jesus' expense. They put upon Him a purple robe and upon His head a crown of thorns, bowing before Him in mock worship. After some time of this mockery and evil treatment at the hands of the soldiers—He had been whipped and further abused—they placed upon His shoulders a cross, and led Him through the streets of Jerusalem up to Golgotha, where He was to be crucified.

Sacrifice (John 19:17-37; Matt. 27:34-53). Jesus Christ, the righteous Son of God, was taken by heathen soldiers and nailed to a rough wooden cross between two thieves on a slight elevation outside the walls of Jerusalem. He hung on the cross from about nine o'clock in the morning till late in the afternoon of the same day. Several important occurrences will be noticed in connection with this time, especially the events surrounding the famous words spoken by Jesus as He suffered on the cross. It would be well to notice each of them. As the act of crucifixion was taking place, Jesus breathed a prayer in behalf of those responsible, saying, "Father, forgive them; for they know not what they do" (Luke 23:34). The second sentence spoken by Jesus on the cross was to the dying thief who penitently asked Jesus to remember him: "To day shalt thou be with me in paradise" (Luke, v. 43). Jesus then made provision for the caring of His mother, by instructing John that he was to care for her (John 19:26, 27). About this time a great darkness covered the area, lasting for three hours (in the middle of the day). The words "My God, my God, why hast thou forsaken me?" (Matt. 27:46) were torn from the lips of Jesus by a great flood of grief over the weight of the sins of the world, which settled down upon Him greatly as the hour of His death drew near. In response to His plea that He was thirsty, He received a sponge containing vinegar (John 19:30; Luke 23:46).

Several natural phenomena also accompanied Christ's suffering on the cross. One was the darkness coming in the middle of the day, already mentioned. At another time—just as Christ gave up the ghost—the veil of the temple was rent in two, the earth quaked, and graves were opened (Matt. 27:51-53).

It is remarkable, too, to consider the number of prophecies which were fulfilled during the time of Christ's trial and crucifixion. Here are just a few: "As a sheep before her shearers is dumb, so he openeth not his mouth" (Isa. 53:7), refers to the fact that Jesus did not defend Himself before His judges. "They part my garments among them, and cast lots upon my vesture," foretold the parting of His garments by the Roman soldiers (Ps. 22:18; Matt. 27:35). "They shall look upon me whom they have pierced" prophesies of the sword thrust in the side of Jesus from which flowed water and blood mixed together (Zech. 12:10; John 19:37). Many other prophecies, far too numerous to mention, were also fulfilled during these few hours of His passion.

The significance of this Man's death is so great that even Christians are at a loss to realize it fully. He went to the cross carrying upon His body the sins of the world—past, present, and future—yet without sin Himself, and offered Himself as a pure blood sacrifice for the remission of those sins. By Christ's obedience and self-sacrifice the whole human race was redeemed from the sentence of death passed upon it by the disobedience of Adam, and by the shedding of the blood of the Son of God we have all gained access to eternal life. The death of Jesus, accompanied by His pain, burden, and grief, was, for that reason, the greatest blessing ever bestowed upon mankind.

Triumph (Luke 23:50-56; John 19:38-42). Late in the afternoon, Joseph of Arimathaea visited the palace of Pilate and acquired permission to take the body of Jesus from the cross. Then, with the help of Nicodemus, he prepared the body of Jesus for burial.[48] In this tomb the body of Jesus lay from Friday evening through the Sabbath day. The Jews got permission from Pilate to place a watch at the tomb, in order that Jesus' disciples might not steal the body and spread the news that He had risen from the dead. The Jews realized that such an occurrence would defeat their purposes utterly, for thus, in death, Christ's cause would blossom even more.

Resurrection Morning (Matt. 28:1-15; Mark 16:1-11). But even an army of soldiers could not have prevented the Son of God from breaking the bonds of death and arising triumphantly from His cruel death. Early in the morning following the Sabbath day, several women came to anoint the body of Jesus, but, to their surprise, they found the stone rolled away from the entrance. Upon entering the sepulchre they were startled to find the body of Jesus gone and an angel sitting there, who informed them that Jesus had risen from the dead. The keepers who had been posted by the priests, after they had recovered from their shock at the miraculous occurrence, went and told the priests what had happened. The priests then bribed the men to claim that they had fallen asleep, which allowed the disciples to steal away the body. This they did, and the Jews even yet declare that such was the true explanation. Jesus, Himself, appeared to Mary Magdalene first, and then to the other women, instructing them to inform the disciples that He would meet them in Galilee.

The Forty Days (Acts. 1:2-4). The period between Jesus' resurrection and His ascension lasted about forty days (Acts 1:3), during which time He appeared quite often and taught His disciples many things concerning Himself and the events of the future. The following, it seems, is the proper sequence of main appearances: appeared to two of the disciples on the way to Emmaus (Mark 16:12, 13); ate with the disciples (Luke 24:36-48); ate again with disciples, proving His reality to Thomas (John 20:26-29); appeared to His disciples in the morning on the seashore after they had fished all night (John 21:1-5); appeared to disciples on the mountain where He gave them the great commission (Mark 16:15-18). This list is almost complete, but the details of each appearance have been left for the student to fill in by reading the accompanying Scripture references.

The Ascension (Acts 1:6-11). Near the end of the forty-day period, Christ led His disciples out as far as Bethany where He lifted up His hands and blessed them. All during His ministry, Christ had made references to the outpouring of the Holy Ghost, but on this occasion He told His disciples that they should not leave Jerusalem until they received the Holy Ghost, after which they should receive such great power as would enable them to evangelize the world. Following His instructions to them concerning the soon-coming event, He was carried up into heaven by a cloud. While they stood gazing after His departing figure, two men stood nearby, who told them, "Ye men of Galilee, why stand ye gazing up into heaven? this same Jesus, which is taken up from you into heaven, shall so come in like manner as ye have seen him go into heaven" (v. 11). Following this amazing and wonderful sequence of events, the Scripture says that they "returned to Jerusalem with great joy" (Luke 24:52).

The Day of Pentecost. *In the Upper Room* (Acts 2:1-36). The disciples of Jesus began to meet regularly and often in the "upper room." What time they were not meeting in this room, they were in the temple worshipping the Lord. It was a time of preparation and a time of expectation. The number of the names of the disciples was one hundred twenty, evidently including the women. But when the day of Pentecost arrived, they were all together in the upper room and in one accord. And as they prayed, a great sound from heaven filled the room and upon each of the disciples appeared cloven tongues like fire. "And they were all filled with the Holy Ghost, and began to speak with other tongues, as the Spirit gave them utterance" (Acts 2:4).[49] At that season of the year, Jerusalem was crowded with Jewish people from all over the world who had come to celebrate the religious holidays. The spectacle of these Galileans speaking in the languages of their homelands so amazed and troubled them that they came together in a great throng and questioned among themselves concerning the meaning of this manifestation. Then Peter, with a new boldness and courage, stood up to face the multitude. In one of the most forceful sermons recorded in the New Testament, he pointed out that this manifestation was not drunkenness, but an outpouring of the Spirit of God in fulfillment of prophecy. He preached to this great gathering of Jews the message of the coming of Christ, His sacrifice, and His return to the Father, which was witnessed by the fact that the Holy Ghost had now been sent.

Witnessing in Jerusalem and Judaea (Acts 2:37-8:1). When Peter had finished speaking, the audience was greatly stirred and began inquiring how that they might be saved. Peter then began to preach repentance for the remission of sins. The results were astounding, for many people believed the word, "and the same day there were added unto them about three thousand souls" (Acts 2:41).

The Correspondence of the Apostle Paul. Paul, no doubt, wrote many other letters than the ones which are included in the books of the New Testament, but they have been lost. Evidently they were not quite so great as the ones which are included in the books of the New Testament. These are thirteen in number which fall into various groupings. Paul was the most prolific writer of his time, having contributed almost half of the books of the Christian Testament. He dealt with nearly every phase of Christian life, giving both the doctrinal and practical aspects of the Christian religion. Too, he was primarily a spiritual man. Paul was educated, but that education was not the thing to which he attributed his success as a minister.

There was a specific purpose behind each letter that he wrote; the epistles were not written merely for the sake of communicating. They were dispatched either in answer to questions or because of certain situations which had arisen.

In the discussion of these books, these reasons for writing will be discussed, since they help the student to understand the epistles.

It is not the purpose of this lesson to exhaust the obtainable information concerning these epistles, nor is space available.[50] In fact, so much of the scholarly research scoffs at the inspired nature of God's Word that it is unedifying to read it. However, the most important points in each book will be given in outline form for the convenience of the student.

Early Epistles to the Churches. Paul preached and labored for several years before he began his writing ministry. Perhaps he had written letters in the period previous to the first missionary journey with Barnabas, but we have no record of them, nor do they exist. Therefore, it is fairly certain that it was about seventeen years before he wrote the first letters which appear in the New Testament. It is generally agreed that the first letters written by him—of those in the New Testament—were the epistles to the Thessalonians, so they will be discussed first.

Epistles to the Thessalonians. Thessalonica was probably the most important city in Macedonia, with the exception of Philippi. After Paul's persecution in Philippi on his second missionary journey, he went to Thessalonica, where he established a church. However, he soon had to flee this city also, due to an uprising of persecution at the hands of the Jews. In the ensuing lapse of time, Paul visited Berea and Athens, from whence Paul sent Timothy to encourage the new brethren in Thessalonica. Timothy returned to find Paul at Corinth, bringing good news of the firmness of the work in Thessalonica. Paul wrote the first epistle from Corinth about a year after he had left the region of Macedonia. Both the first and second epistles are built around Paul's teaching concerning the second coming of Christ, the second epistle especially.

The main points of 1 Thessalonians are as follows:

1. Paul commends the church for its faithfulness (ch. 1).
2. Paul clears himself of false charges (ch. 2).
3. Paul gives instruction (ch. 3-5).
   a. Practical admonitions to observe the Christian virtues of love, holiness, industry, sympathy, and patience, and to avoid even the appearance of evil (3:12-4:11; 5:5-22).

b. Doctrine of the second coming of Christ, given to comfort those mourning departed love ones (4:13-5:4).

Numbers of the early saints somehow received the mistaken impression that the Lord was coming in a few days. Undoubtedly this came from the strong exhortations to be ready for that coming, which they interpreted to mean that He was coming in their lifetime. The saints at Thessalonica, after receiving Paul's first letter and gathering from his instructions that Christ was coming any moment, left off working and began to sit around in groups waiting for the expected event. When this came to Paul's ears, he wrote the second epistle to correct their mistaken impressions. The second letter was written within a short time—certainly within a year—after the first one.

The most important parts of 2 Thessalonians are the following:

1. Paul congratulates their stability in the gospel, admonishing them to grow in grace (ch. 1).
2. Paul corrects their errors concerning the second coming of Jesus by pointing out (ch. 2):
   a. That the falling away must come first (2:2-3).
   b. The antichrist will be made manifest (2:3-8).
   c. He and his followers will be destroyed before the second coming (2:8-12).
3. Paul points out several duties of the church (ch. 3).

Since the doctrine of the second coming of Christ is most important element about the two books, it might worthwhile to point out some of the more important teaching about this event. Paul tells us that Christ is surely to come back in person. It will also be sudden and unexpected, which reason we should always be ready for it. To those are ready it will be a glorious time.

Galatians. This letter was written not to any one but to a group of churches. In fact, all the churches sizable region of Galatia in that part of the world known as Asia. You will notice that Paul first region of Galatia on his second journey. It was established the churches to which he wrote the people of the area had quickly accepted the gospel preached, but as in other places as soon as teachers came along behind him and attempt to what he had built. People came to Galatia with the same harsh doctrine which had occasioned the council in Jerusalem: they taught the new Gentile converts that it was necessary for them to be circumcised after the Mosaic law or they could not be saved. In addition to spreading this teaching, they tried to strengthen their words by claiming that the other apostles, to whom they claimed Paul was inferior, taught circumcision, and that even Paul was not consistent in his teaching concerning the Mosaic law. Thus it is that the first part of the epistle to the Galatians is spent by the apostle in vindicating himself from the false charges, while the second portion contains certain things taken from the Old Testament, which go a long way toward proving that the ceremonies of the law were abolished by Jesus Christ.

The main points of the Galatians are as follows:

I. Vindication of himself and his doctrine (ch. 1; 2)
   A. Paul asserts his right to the claim of apostleship (1:11-24)
   B. Paul preaches same doctrine as other apostles (2:1-10)
   C. Paul practices what he preaches (2:11-21)

II. Proof of the abrogation of the ceremonial law (ch.3; 4)
   A. Justification by faith (ch. 3)
   B. Freedom from the law (4:1-20)
   C. Allegory of Sarah and Hagar (4:21-31)

III. Instructions of a practical nature (ch. 5: 6)
   A. Paul admonishes to maintain freedom in Christ (5:1-12)
   B. However, "use not liberty for an occasion to the flesh" (5:13-6:17)

Epistles to the Corinthians. Corinth was a Greek city in the province of Achaia, situated on the narrow neck of land which connects the Peloponnesus to the mainland of Greece. Its geographic position greatly facilitated its use as a trading port bringing to its inhabitants much prosperity in the time of Paul. However, it was this very prosperity which made of the Corinthian populace a people steeped in all manner of sin and vice. Paul first visited this city on the second missionary journey, after he had answered the Macedonian call by going from Asia Minor to the Grecian territory. Even among the super abundance of paganism and ungodliness, Paul established a fairly large church, mostly of converts from paganism, although undoubtedly a few of the dispersed Jews were among the number. The first epistle was written from Ephesus, probably about three years after he had departed from the newly-founded church in Corinth, and was designed to correct various disorders which had arisen in the church, as well as to answer some specific questions previously asked him.

After a typical Pauline introduction occupying about three verses, the following points of 1 Corinthians are the most significant:

1. An exhortation to unity and harmony (1:4-16)
2. Glory in the power of God and not in the flesh (1:16-4:21)
3. A reproof for not disfellowshiping fornicators (5:1-13), and for going to law against each other and that before heathen judges (6:1-11)
4. Admonition to abstain from fornication (6:12-20)
5. Instructions on marriage, in answer to their questions (ch. 7)
6. Instructions on eating meats offered to idols in which Paul expounds on Christian liberty (ch. 8)
7. Hire for the minister's labor (9:1-14)
8. Nothing displeasing to God and all to His glory (ch. 10)
9. Admonition for women to refrain from cutting their hair (11:4-16)
10. Admonition against profaning the Lord's Supper (11:18-34)
11. Spiritual gifts (ch. 12-14)
12. The Resurrection (15:58)

The last chapter is one of historical interest. It concerns the collection for the saints at Jerusalem and contains instructions from Paul as to the details of the collection; he also traces for his readers the route he is to take before the collection is finally delivered to the needy saints in Jerusalem. This is part of the route of the third missionary journey, which we studied in the last lesson.

The second epistle was written from the city of Philippi in the region of Macedonia within a year's time after the first. This letter was sent by Paul after he had received a report from Titus concerning the results of his first epistle. This report was, for the most part, a cheering one, for the Corinthian church had given heed to the advice of its "spiritual parent," and was earnestly striving to correct the evils which had sprung up. However, some trouble with false teachers had again reared its ugly head, being strengthened by certain ones arriving in Corinth with a claim to a higher authority than that of Paul. The undertone of Paul's indignation against these people is apparent throughout the second epistle. (See 5:12, 13.) But mostly the second letter commends their giving heed to his former instructions, saying, "Now I rejoice . . . that ye sorrowed to repentance" (7:9). This rejoicing, along with many sincere exhortations, takes up the first seven chapters. Chapters 8 and 9 are concerned mostly with the collection for the saints at Jerusalem which was mentioned in the other letter, admonishing them not to be slothful in this matter and pointing out the benefits of giving. The last four chapters are a little more firm in admonishing them to keep the faith; again Paul takes up his defense against those who were in Corinth attempting to destroy his influence.

Romans. The book of Romans is considered by many to be the greatest of Paul's epistles inasmuch as it contains almost the totality of what must have been his basic message to the Gentile world. It was written from Corinth approximately a year after 2 Corinthians, in which time Paul had fulfilled his promise to revisit the Corinthians. Rome was the capital city of the empire, the seat of Roman government and authority. The Church of God there had not been established by Paul, but it was a thriving church. It is not known by whom the church was established, nor when, but Paul had a desire to preach the gospel in Rome as he had done elsewhere.

Paul's purpose in writing the letter is not clearly defined. Undoubtedly it was a letter of introduction preparatory to his expected visit. But it must have been more than that. He presents to his unknown Roman audience the doctrine that he had preached elsewhere. Undoubtedly the Roman church had heard of Paul and his preaching, but, in all probability, many misunderstood the great apostle's message. Probably Paul had this in mind also when he wrote this letter to them. But most of all, in view of the inspiration of God, it must be understood that God's hand was behind every move of the apostle and that this was no exception. God had specific things which the Romans should hear and which must come from Paul. Too, God, in His infinite wisdom and farsightedness, could see that this grand statement of the Christian doctrine would prove a blessing to countless thousands of believers down through the ages.

Its central theme is the liberty of the Christian religion in its emphasis on grace and faith, rather than the works of the law. He deals at great length on the Jewish law, but merely to point out in what fashion Christ had fulfilled it. The book is divided into two main divisions. The first portion, containing eleven chapters, is theological and doctrinal; the last five chapters are of a practical nature. The main points of Romans are as follows:

I. Doctrinal
   A. Justification by faith in Jesus Christ and not by works (ch. 1-4); peace with God, sanctification, glorification (ch. 5-8)
   B. Clarification and defense of justification by faith without the works of the law, and the admission of Gentiles into the church without circumcision (ch. 9-11)
II. Practical
   A. Exhortations to observe necessary Christian duties (ch. 12)
   B. Instructions on obedience to civil authority (ch. 13)
   C. Relations between Christians (ch. 14-15:14)
   D. Various personal greetings and conclusion (15:15-16:27)

In the fifteenth chapter Paul traces his proposed plans for going to Jerusalem to deliver to them the collection which has occupied so much of his energy and thought for quite some time, after which he plans to visit them on his way to preach the gospel in Spain.

Prison Epistles. Romans was the last letter written by Paul as a free man. All the rest of his letters which have been preserved for us were written from his Roman imprisonment; hence, the designation "prison epistles." Approximately three years elapsed from the time of his writing to the Romans until he arrived in that city—as the emperor's prisoner.

Colossians. This letter was written to the church at Colosse, a city of greater Phrygia, not far from the city of Laodicea. Paul, even though he had evangelized the major portion of Phrygia, had never visited the saints there. The church had probably been organized by Epaphras, who was present with Paul when this epistle was written. The city of

Colosse was destroyed by the Emperor Nero a few years after the martyrdom of Paul.

The Colossians had been visited by some false teachers who attempted to introduce certain Jewish and heathen practices and doctrines into the purity of their faith and practice. They appear to have taught, in opposition to the doctrine of the apostles, that the angels were the only mediators between God and man and that only by certain rituals, taken mainly from the Jewish law, could these angels be induced to intercede in their behalf. Thus the purpose of this letter was to prevent the saints from falling into the error of Jewish ritualism and pagan superstition. The central theme of the book is that Christ is all-sufficient as the Lord of the universe and the Head of the Church.

The main points of Colossians are as follows:

I.   Doctrinal, in which Paul explains the mystery of Christ (1:3-8)

II. Exhortation (ch. 2-4)
    A. Paul admonishes them to be persistent, and warns them against deception (1:9-2:15)
    B. Paul describes, in more detail, the mystery of Christ (2:16-3:4)
       1. Mystery of the Church, with Christ as the Head (2:16-19)
       2. Mystery of His death (2:20-23)
       3. Mystery of His resurrection and glorification (3:1-4)
    C. Paul exhorts the saints about specific things (3:5-4:18)

Summing it up in a sentence or two, we find that Paul recommends the knowledge of Jesus Christ as all-sufficient, eliminating any necessity for the intercession of angels. He further establishes that Christ is far superior to the angels, who are really only His servants, and that it is through Him that we have contact with God and access to His promises.

Philemon. This is a short personal note written also to Colosse, but addressed directly to Philemon. It is counted as the second of Paul's prison epistles and concerns a purely private matter. Onesimus, a servant (or slave) of Philemon, had run away from his master, eventually arriving in Rome. Here he came under the influence of the apostle Paul, who was instrumental in converting him to Christianity, and who persuaded him to return voluntarily to his master, who was also a Christian. The letter was sent along with Onesimus on his return journey.

In this letter, Paul, as in other of his letters, teaches that the Christian must be subject to civil law, which, in this instance, demanded that Onesimus return to his master. Paul instructs Philemon to treat the returning slave with Christian love, to receive him as a brother in Christ.[51] Paul does not denounce the practice of slavery, but by his insistence upon the manifestation of love paves the way for its peaceful destruction. This letter, although it contains no violent abolitionist ideas, is considered by some as the first antislavery tract.

Ephesians. Ephesus was the principal city in the coastal region of the Roman province of Asia. The Apostle Paul had preached here for three years (Acts 19:8-22); here the memorable conflict with the enraged silversmiths took place. From the church at Ephesus the gospel spread throughout the whole region. While Paul was at Miletus on the return leg of his third journey, he warned the elders of the Ephesian church, who had come there in answer to his call, that severe persecutions would surely arise from the unbelievers, and that false and destructive teachers would also arise in their midst. He wrote this epistle, which was intended for circulation among quite a few of the churches in Asia Minor, to keep them firmly in the faith and to provide them with a spiritual defense against false teachers. It probably was written at the same time as the epistle to the Colossians so that it could be delivered in Ephesus by Tychicus who must pass through Ephesus on his way to Colosse. The theme of the book is the union of God's holy Church to Christ as its Head.

The principal elements of Ephesians are the following:

I. Statement of the doctrine (ch. 1-3)
   A. Election and adoption of grace (1:1-14)
   B. Abolishment of the middle wall of partition (ch. 2)
   C. Fellowship of the mystery (ch. 3)
II. Exhortation (ch. 4-6)
   A. Unity of the faith (4:1-16)
   B. Comparison between Christian Gentiles and pagans (4:17-24)
   C. Evils to avoid (4: 25-5:21)
   D. Mystery of Christ and the Church as husband and wife (5:22-23)

E. Duties of parents and children, servants, and masters (6:1-9)

F. The good fight of faith (6:10-20)

Philippians. Paul's first visit to Philippi was in answer to an extraordinary call—that of the vision of the man from Macedonia. At Philippi Paul endured many persecutions—remember the Philippian jail—yet he managed to obtain a few converts. While the beginnings of the Philippian church were small, he did not become discouraged for he had been expressly sent there by God. Evidently the church later became a prosperous one, for theirs was the only church who sent support to him while he was imprisoned at Rome (4:15). The letter was written some eleven years after the church had been organized by Paul and was sent in answer to expressions of sympathy and a gift which had been brought from Philippi by Epaphroditus. The dominant theme of the book is "joy," a word often repeated during these four short chapters.

The main points of Philippians are as follows:

I. Joy despite imprisonment (1:12-24).
   A. Paul exhorts them to continue in the faith while he lives (1:25-2:16)
   B. Even if he should die, Paul exhorts them to rejoice with him (2:17, 18)

II. Further exhortation to rejoice (3:1-3)
   A. Paul exhorts them to beware of false teachers (3:1-3)
   B. Paul exhorts them to keep the righteousness they had been taught (4:1-9)
   C. Paul accepts their liberal offering (4:10-23)

Pastoral Epistles. The three letters under this heading are called such because they are primarily advice given for a pastor or a "shepherd of a spiritual flock." All of them were written during Paul's imprisonment at Rome.

The Epistles to Timothy. Timothy was the son of a Jewess and a Greek father. He was brought up in the knowledge of the Scriptures by his devout mother and grandmother and was converted under the preaching of Paul, probably at Lystra. He later became one of Paul's most faithful companions on his missionary trips, and eventually was appointed by Paul to be the overseer of Ephesus. This was his position at the time of the writing of the two epistles bearing his name.

The first epistle was written with the purpose of giving Timothy instructions in his office as bishop and, through him, to pass on certain instructions to the churches under his care.

The main points of 1 Timothy are as follows:

1. Qualifications of bishops and deacons (ch. 3)
2. Details of the apostasy (ch. 4)
3. Rules to observe in reproving elders, caring for widows, being impartial in everything (ch. 5)
4. Instructions to servants, warning concerning the love of money (ch. 6)

The second epistle to Timothy was written approximately two years after the first, and Paul's purpose was to inform Timothy of his approaching death and to ask him to come quickly to Rome.

The main points of 2 Timothy are as follows:

1. Paul exhorts Timothy to "Endure hardness as a good soldier" (ch. 2)
2. Paul foretells the apostasy (ch. 3:1- 4:4)
3. Paul hints that his "good fight of faith" is about over and desires Timothy to make haste to come to him (4:5-22)

Titus. This great Christian worker was converted under Paul's ministry and helped in the establishment of the Macedonian churches. He was, by Paul's authority, the overseer of the churches in Crete. The epistle to him, the aim of which was to aid him in the difficult work of regulating the Cretan churches, was written shortly after the first epistle to Timothy, both of which are strikingly similar.

The most important points of Titus are these:

1. Ordaining qualified men as bishops (ch. 1)
2. Instructions on sound doctrine, (ch. 2)
3. Civil obedience (3:1-7)
4. Maintaining good works, avoiding vain questions, dealing with heretics (3:8-11)

General Epistle to the Hebrews. This letter is addressed to a Jewish audience. Most were written to individual Gentiles or to Gentile churches, although these churches undoubtedly contained a liberal sprinkling of Jewish converts. The Epistle to the Hebrews is addressed to the Jews of the dispersion, those Jews who were scattered abroad in every portion of the Roman empire.

Hebrews was written for a group of Christian Jews wavering between Christianity and Judaism. It is in a sense the counterpart to Paul's letter to the Romans, this time directed to a Jewish audience and explaining Christ's relationship to all that had gone before in the religious history of Israel.[52]

Many believe that Paul is the author of this epistle even though his name does not appear in the letter itself. The writer of this book quotes many of the same verses of Scripture (Heb. 2:8; 10:30, 38), and employs similar expressions as are found in other of his letters. Evidently, from what internal evidence this book contains, it was written before the destruction of the temple, which occurred in A.D. 70.

This book was written to point out that Christ was the divine fulfillment of the Mosaic law. It is a sublime statement that the old covenant has been abrogated by a new and better covenant, of which Jesus Christ is the High Priest. It points out that although all the angels, prophets, and Old Testament figures were great, Jesus Christ is immeasurably greater. It also teaches us that although God's people under the old dispensations had enjoyed great blessings, the people of God under the grace dispensation are even more favored. Too, there can be seen a great contrast between faith and observance of the law, with Abraham being pointed out as the "father of the faithful."

The broad outline of Hebrews is as follows:

1. Christ is superior to angels (ch. 1, 2)
2. Jesus Christ, as mediator of the new covenant, is superior to Moses, the mediator of the law (ch. 3, 4)
3. Christ is our High Priest, is everlasting, is perfect, made the final and perfect sacrifice (ch. 5-10)
4. Greater necessity for faith is laid upon us (ch. 11)
5. The author exhorts readers to patience, godliness, and steadfastness (ch. 12)
6. The author gives practical application for godly conduct (ch. 13)

Objective: The individual will demonstrate an understanding of the content of the New Testament by constructing a chronological outline of the main events in the life of Christ.

Bible Training Institute, General Bible Study,
pp. 112, 122, 132

I.   John the Baptist
    A. Birth and Life
    B. Ministry
       1. Location and Duration
       2. His Message
    C. His Position in Relation to the Messiah

II. Early Life of Jesus
    A. Birth and Genealogy
    B. Incidents in Early Life
    C. Baptism in Jordan

III. Preparation and Time of Obscurity
    A. The Temptation (Matt. 4:1-11)
    B. First Miracle (John 2:1-11)
    C. Meeting With Nicodemus (John 3:1-21)
    D. The Samaritan Woman (John 4:5-42)

IV. Time of Popular Favor
    A. Sermon on the Mount (Matt. 5-7)
    B. Healing of Woman With Issue of Blood (Mark 5:22-34)

V.   Time of Opposition
    A. Feeding of Five Thousand (Mark 6:35-44)
    B. Divinity of Jesus (Matt. 16:13-20)
    C. Transfiguration (Luke 9:28-36)
    D. Healing of Ten Lepers (Luke 17:11-19)
    E. Raising of Lazarus (John 11:1-46)

VI. Beginning of Passion Week
    A. Triumphal Entry
    B. Predictions Concerning Death
    C. Other Events

Bible Training Institute, *General Bible Study,* (Cleveland, TN: White Wing Publishing House, 1976), pp. 112, 122, 132. Used by permission.

VII. Upper Room and the Garden
    A. Lord's Supper and Feet-washing
    B. The Traitor
    C. The Garden

VIII. Trial and Crucifixion
    A. The Sanhedrin
    B. Pilate
    C. Sacrifice

IX. Triumph
    A. Resurrection Morning
    B. The Forty Days
    C. Ascension

Objective: The individual will demonstrate an understanding of the content of the New Testament by tracing on a map the missionary journeys of the apostle Paul.

PAUL'S FIRST MISSIONARY JOURNEY

"So when they had appointed elders in every church, and prayed with fasting, they commended them to the Lord in whom they had believed." —Acts 14:23

Paul preaches; Jewish leaders oppose gospel (Acts 13:16 ff.).

Many believe; persecution arises (Acts 14:1 ff.).

Paul and Barnabas called gods; Paul stoned (Acts 14:8 ff.).

Paul, Barnabas and Mark sail for Cyprus (Acts 13:4).

Mark leaves (Acts 13:13).

Proconsul Sergius Paulus believes; sorcerer Elymas blinded (Acts 13:7 ff.).

outward leg
return leg

Euphrates River

GALATIA   CAPPADOCIA

SYRIA

Antioch
Seleucia

Tarsus
CILICIA

LYCAONIA
Iconium
Derbe
Lystra
Pisidian Antioch
Perga

Mediterranean Sea

CYPRUS   Salamis
Paphos

MYSIA

Pergamos
Thyatira Sardis PHRYGIA
Smyrna Ephesus Philadelphia
Laodicea
Colosse
Miletus
LYCIA Attalia
PATMOS
COS
RHODES

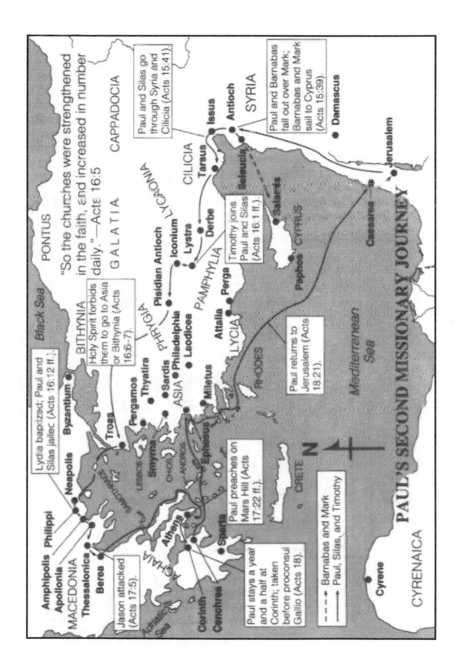

PAUL'S SECOND MISSIONARY JOURNEY

"So the churches were strengthened in the faith, and increased in number daily." —Acts 16:5

Paul and Silas go through Syria and Cilicia (Acts 15:41).

Paul and Barnabas fall out over Mark; Barnabas and Mark sail to Cyprus (Acts 15:39).

Timothy joins Paul and Silas (Acts 16:1 ff.).

Paul returns to Jerusalem (Acts 18:21).

Holy Spirit forbids them to go to Asia or Bithynia (Acts 16:6-7).

Lydia baptized; Paul and Silas jailed (Acts 16:12 ff.).

Paul preaches on Mars Hill (Acts 17:22 ff.).

Jason attacked (Acts 17:5).

Paul stays a year and a half at Corinth; taken before proconsul Gallio (Acts 18).

- - - → Barnabas and Mark
——→ Paul, Silas, and Timothy

Black Sea

PONTUS

CAPPADOCIA

GALATIA

BITHYNIA

PHRYGIA

LYCAONIA

Pisidian Antioch

Iconium

Lystra

Derbe

PAMPHYLIA

Perga

Attalia

LYCIA

SYRIA

Antioch

Issus

CILICIA

Tarsus

Seleucia

Salamis

CYPRUS

Paphos

Damascus

Jerusalem

Caesarea

Mediterranean Sea

RHODES

CRETE

ASIA

Miletus

Ephesus

Smyrna

Sardis

Thyatira

Philadelphia

Leodicea

Pergamos

Troas

Neapolis

Byzantium

Philippi

Amphipolis

Apollonia

MACEDONIA

Thessalonica

Berea

ACHAIA

Athens

Corinth

Cenchrea

Sparta

Adriatic Sea

CYRENAICA

Cyrene

N

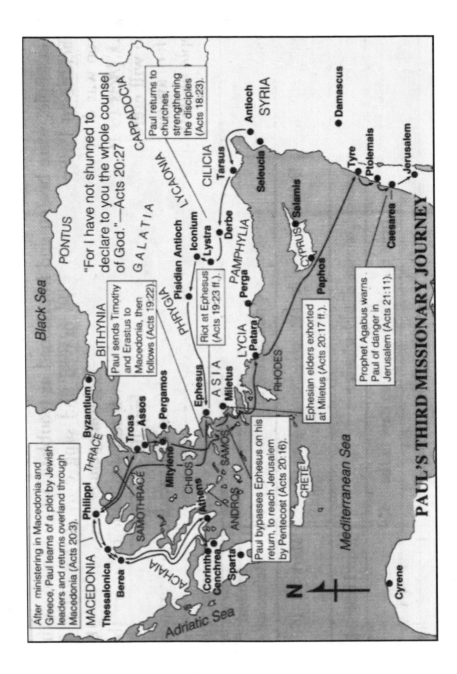

PAUL'S THIRD MISSIONARY JOURNEY

"For I have not shunned to declare to you the whole counsel of God." —Acts 20:27

After ministering in Macedonia and Greece, Paul learns of a plot by Jewish leaders and returns overland through Macedonia (Acts 20:3).

Paul sends Timothy and Erastus to Macedonia, then follows (Acts 19:22).

Paul returns to churches, strengthening the disciples (Acts 18:23).

Riot at Ephesus (Acts 19:23 ff.).

Ephesian elders exhorted at Miletus (Acts 20:17 ff.).

Paul bypasses Ephesus on his return, to reach Jerusalem by Pentecost (Acts 20:16).

Prophet Agabus warns Paul of danger in Jerusalem (Acts 21:11).

Black Sea

Mediterranean Sea

Adriatic Sea

PONTUS

CAPPADOCIA

LYCAONIA

GALATIA

CILICIA

SYRIA

Damascus

Antioch

Tarsus

Seleucia

Tyre

Ptolemais

Jerusalem

Caesarea

CYPRUS

Salamis

Paphos

PAMPHYLIA

Perga

Patara

LYCIA

RHODES

PHRYGIA

Pisidian Antioch

Iconium

Lystra

Derbe

ASIA

Ephesus

Miletus

SAMOS

CHIOS

ANDROS

CRETE

Pergamos

Assos

Troas

Mitylene

SAMOTHRACE

THRACE

Byzantium

BITHYNIA

MACEDONIA

Philippi

Thessalonica

Berea

ACHAIA

Athens

Corinth

Cenchrea

Sparta

Cyrene

N

Objective: The individual will demonstrate an understanding of the content of the New Testament by naming the Beatitudes.

Holy Bible, Matthew 5:1-12

And seeing the multitudes, he want up into a mountain: and when he was set, his disciples came unto him:
And he opened his mouth, and taught them, saying,
Blessed are the poor in spirit: for theirs is the kingdom of heaven.
Blessed are they that mourn: for they shall be comforted.
Blessed are the meek: for they shall inherit the earth.
Blessed are they which do hunger and thirst after righteousness: for they shall be filled.
Blessed are the merciful: for they shall obtain mercy.
Blessed are the pure in heart: for they shall see God.
Blessed are the peacemakers: for they shall be called the children of God.
Blessed are they which are persecuted for righteousness' sake: for theirs is the kingdom of heaven.
Blessed are ye, when men shall revile you, and persecute you, and shall say all manner of evil against you falsely, for my sake.
Rejoice, and be exceeding glad: for great is your reward in heaven: for so persecuted they the prophets which were before you.

ENDNOTES

[1] From John Wesley's *Journal,* (Chicago: Moody Press).

[2] Author unknown.

[3] Louis Gaussen, *Theopneustia: The Plenary Inspiration of the Holy Scriptures* (Chicago: The Bible Institute, 1949).

[4] F. F. Bruce, *The Books and the Parchments* (Westwood, NJ: Revell, 1963), p. 45.

[5] Norman L. Geisler and William E. Nix, *A General Introduction to the Bible* (Chicago: Moody, 1968), p. 19.

[6] Wycliffe's first English Bible followed the fourfold division that was used in the Vulgate Bible.

[7] This section is taken from Raymond M. Pruitt, *Fundamentals of the Faith* (Cleveland, TN: White Wing, 1981), p. 28.

[8] B. F. Westcott, *A General Survey of the History of the Canon of the New Testament* (New York: Macmillan, 1896), p. 456.

[9] Geisler and Nix, op. cit., p. 195.

[10] George Salmon, *A Historical Introduction to the Study of the Books of the New Testament* (London: John Murray, 1888), p. 121. Italics ours.

[11] Edward J. Young, "The Canon of the Old Testament," in *Revelation and the Bible,* ed. Carl F. H. Henry (Grand Rapids: Baker, 1958), p. 156.

[12] Geisler and Nix, op. cit., p. 136.

[13] During the period of the old and middle English, only portions of Scripture were translated from old Latin and the Vulgate Bible. Among some of the notables who translated some Scripture passages were: Caedmon, narratives of Genesis, Exodus, Daniel; Aldhelm translated the Psalter; Egbert translated the Synoptic Gospels; the Venerable Bede, the Gospel of John; Alfred the Great, the Ten Commandments; Ormin paraphrased the Gospels and Acts; and Richard Rolle produced a literal translation of the Psalter.

[14] Geisler and Nix, *op. cit.,* p. 406.

[15] This classification is based on that used in Jesse Lyman Hurlbut, *Hurlbut's Teacher-Training Lessons* (New York: Abingdon-Cokesbury, 1908), and is used by permission.

[16]"It is said to be in Mesopotamia, or more definitely in Padan-Aram, the cultivated district at the foot of the hills, a name well applying to the beautiful stretch of country which lies below Mount Masius between the Khabour and the Euphrates. Here, about midway in this district, is a small village still called HARAN." William Smith, *A Dictionary of the Bible*, ed. F. N. and M. A. Peloubet (Peabody, MA: Hendrickson, n. d.).

[17]Melchizedek is one of the most obscure figures in Bible history. He appears mysteriously from nowhere, and then fades again into complete oblivion. Hebrews 7:1-3 says, "For this Melchizedek, king of Salem, priest of the most high God, who met Abraham returning from the slaughter of the kings, and blessed him; To whom also Abraham gave a tenth part of all; first being by interpretation King of righteousness, and after that also King of Salem, which is, King of peace; Without father, without mother, without descent, having neither beginning of days, nor end of life. . . ." Christ, Himself, is an high priest after the order of Melchizedek. (Read Heb. 5:1-10 and Heb. 7.)

[18]Notice that the name is no longer Abram, for God had changed his name (Gen. 17:1-8).

[19]Christ used Lot's wife as an excellent example of people being unable to forget the attractions of the world, those who, having put their hand to plow, look back (Luke 9:62). "Remember Lot's wife" is one of the classic warnings in the New Testament (Luke 17:28-32).

[20]This sacrifice teaches sacrifice and substitution as the way God has planned for the remission of sins. It teaches, too, the necessity for men to be faithful and obedient in order to receive the benefit (Heb. 11:17). The animal substituted is recognized as a type of Christ, who was made a substitute for us, dying on the cross, not for His sin (for He had none), but for our sin. Isaac represents that humanity which was saved from certain death by the sacrifice of Christ.

[21]He had another name—Edom—which mean "red" and, thus, he is the father of the Edomites, who appear time after time as the perpetual enemies of the Israelites.

[22]"It was a pasture land, especially suited to a shepherd people, and sufficient for the Israelites, who prospered, and were separate from the main body of the Egyptians." Peloubet and Smith, *op. cit.*

²³Moses was born of the tribe of Levi, the tribe which later became the priestly family of the Jewish people. He is sometimes called the "Greatest Man in the Old Testament," and he is mentioned approximately eighty times in the New Testament.

²⁴People today also make excuses. Notice the excuses given by Moses and see if they do not sound like some of ours. "Who am I, that I should go unto Pharaoh?" (Exod. 3:11); "What shall I say?" (Exod. 3:13); "They will not believe me" (Exod. 4:1); "I am not eloquent" (Exod. 4:10-17). Just as God would not accept the excuses of Moses, He will not accept ours. No alibi will meet God's approval.

²⁵The sojourn in Egypt was prophesied by the Lord to Abraham (Gen. 15:13, 14). This prophecy was literally fulfilled when the Israelites came up out of Egypt as it is explained in Exod. 12:40, 41.

²⁶It is interesting to note why the Israelites desired a king. They said, "Give us a king. . . like all the nations" (1 Sam. 8:5, 6). They were not willing to be a separate, different people, even though they were God's chosen nation. Notice too, that by setting up a kingdom, they rejected theocratic rule and changed to the rule of man. God yielded to their desires, not because He was pleased, but because they were determined to do so (8:19-22).

²⁷In Samuel's rebuke to Saul, he spoke some of the most often-repeated words in Christian circles. "To obey is better than sacrifice, and to hearken than the fat of rams" (1 Sam. 15:12-23).

²⁸When he was called by God, Jeremiah answered, "I cannot speak: for I am a child" (Jer. 1:6). However, the Lord told him not to worry over his youthfulness because wherever God sent him, He would be with him. This is a lesson to us never to question the call of God despite the apparent foolishness of it. If God calls us to work, then He will provide the means, and what is impossible with us is possible with God. Young people, as well as mature adults, can work for God and can be great soul-winners for His kingdom.

²⁹Read Ezek. 2:3-8. Here God tells Ezekiel that he must preach the Word, regardless of opposition, regardless of unbelief. Just because his hearers might reject the message and rebel was no reason that the prophet should rebel and refuse to deliver the message unto them.

[30]Ezekiel 33, gives the duty of the divine watchmen. If the watchman (in other words, the minister) does not warn the people, then their blood will be upon his hands. When the minister speaks and people hear, then he has benefited his hearers. If they do not hear, then he has discharged his duty. It is his duty to preach the Word, regardless of whether it is accepted or rejected.

[31]Notice that the work of the rebuilding of the wall went quickly because "the people had a mind to work" (Neh. 4:6). This is the kind of spirit needed to get the work of the Lord accomplished.

[32]Daniel, Hananiah, Mishael, and Azariah had their names changed, respectively, to Belteshazzar, Shadrach, Meshach, and Abednego (Dan. 1:7).

[33]Baptism in water is definitely a New Testament teaching. It will be noticed that the word itself means a "dipping," a complete immersion. Andy other practice, regardless of what it might be called, cannot be baptism. Since baptism is an immersion, it was necessary for John to have "much water" (John 3:23). Other verses of Scripture supporting baptism are Matthew 28:19; Mark 1:8-10; Acts 8:38.

[34]Repentance is the very first step in becoming justified before God and is absolutely necessary for salvation. Repentance implies true sorrow for sins committed, a feeling of guilt before God, and a deep conviction of the need of God's forgiveness. Read Luke 13:3 and Acts 3:19.

[35]Capernaum is located on the northwestern coast of the Sea of Galilee. It was the headquarters of Jesus and His disciples during most of His three-year ministry. While not a very large city, it had a synagogue, a Roman custom house, and a contingent of Roman soldiers stationed there. Many of the Lord's miracles of healing were performed either in the city itself or in the immediate vicinity.

[36]John is the only one of the four Gospels which records this early episode of Jesus chasing out the moneychangers and the merchants who were making of the temple a house of merchandise. According to the accounts in the Synoptic Gospels, a similar event occurred near the end of Jesus' ministry on His last visit to Jerusalem before His crucifixion.

[37]Being born again is a definite spiritual experience which comes as the result of repentance and faith. Since Adam,

every human being is spiritually dead from birth. Thus, in order to renew that spiritual life, the experience of being born again is necessary. This is a work of grace wrought in the heart of man whereby "old things are passed away; behold, all things are become new" (2 Cor. 5:7). Read John 3:3; 1 Peter 1:23; 1 John 3:9.

[38]You will notice that, in reality, more than the number mentioned in the Scripture were fed, since the number estimated did not include women and children. Too, it is sometimes overlooked that Jesus performed two miracles like this. At another time, He fed 4,000 (Mark 8:1-9).

[39]He took only three—Peter, James, and John. It is supposed that the Mount of Transfiguration was Mount Hermon, north of Caesarea Philippi, the highest mountain in Palestine.

[40]It is interesting to note that Jesus, in several instances, used a Samaritan to teach a lesson. The parable of the good Samaritan and the woman at the well are examples.

[41]Evidently Judas had been a faithful follower of Christ, but little by little had lost his zeal for the cause. He, undoubtedly from selfish motives, expected Christ to set up a kingdom in which he would have an important position. When he realized that this was not Christ's intention, he seized his opportunity to avenge himself for such a great disappointment.

[42]That some form of church organization had already been instituted is intimated by the fact that Judas was the treasurer. The apostles were already carrying out the functions of the church, as we can see in John 13:29.

[43]The student may become confused unless he realizes there are two cities known as Antioch. The Antioch in this instance is the city of Syria. Later on, Paul visits Antioch in the region of Pisidia, referred to in the lesson as Pisidian Antioch.

[44]John Mark, for some reason, parted from the party in Perga, returning to Jerusalem (Acts 13:13). This departure occurred immediately after the first opposition which they had encountered from the Jews in their journey. Probably this was the reason that Paul did not want to take Mark along on their second journey (15:37, 38).

[45]The Roman Church maintains that the Church was built upon the rock of Peter. But this very instance proves the

instability of any church built upon that "rock." "Peter" means a small rock, a portion of a larger rock. He was only one of the foundation stones, not the foundation itself.

[46]A Roman Catholic Church legend holds Peter to be the first bishop of Rome, and, therefore, the first pope. However, there is no evidence that Peter was ever the leading spirit in the local church at Rome. It cannot be proven that he never visited Rome, but it is certain that he could not have been there very long. The Roman Church classes Peter as the "ruler" of the other apostles, but this could not have been the case.

[47]We are prone to criticize Peter for his denial of Christ, when, in reality, he was no more unfaithful than the other disciples. They all declared that they would not deny Him; yet when the test came, they all fled, denying Him in deed although not in word. Peter did get close enough to Christ for the temptation to arise—to which he yielded, yet he was no more guilty than the rest. Read Matt. 26:35 and 56.

[48]His burial in this fashion fulfilled prophecy. Read Isa. 53:9.

[49]The manifestations of the Holy Ghost on the Day of Pentecost point out what effect His indwelling has upon a human being. That this phenomenon of "speaking in other tongues" accompanied the outpouring of the Holy Ghost upon others is a pretty conclusive sign that such a manifestation is the witness that a person has received the Holy Ghost. Without it how can one know that the Holy Ghost has come? Since the Holy Ghost cannot dwell in an unclean temple, the baptism must come subsequent to the experience of entire sanctification.

[50]Sources for the information in this lesson, besides the Bible, which is the main source, were John Wesley's *Explanatory Notes on the New Testament* and *The People's Bible Encyclopedia.*

[51]Onesimus must have later been given his freedom by Philemon, for Early Church history records that he succeeded Timothy as the overseer of Ephesus.

[52]Alexander, David, and Pat Alexander, ed., *Eerdman's Handbook to the Bible* (Grand Rapids: Eerdmans, 1983) p. 626.

FOUNDATIONS COURSE: The Bible

Registration Form for: Ministers, Ministerial Candidates, *Authorized and Certified Teacher Candidates

Name: _____

Address: _____

_____

Local Church: _____

Pastor: _____

In order to earn a Certificate of Completion or Leadership Development Unit the ministerial candidate should register with the state/regional/national office. The following criteria must be met:

- The ministerial candidate must be approved by the Overseer.
- The ministerial participant must complete the course of study in a reasonable time.
- The approved CBL text must be read and the accompanying examination and assignments successfully completed with a score of 95% (open-book test). The Examination should be sent to the state/regional/ national office for grading.

I am a candidate for:
    ❒ Minister's License   ❒ ~~Authorized Teacher~~ *
    ❒ Certified Teacher   ❒ Minister Upgrading

Please indicate which of the following you are requesting credit for:
    ❒ LDU Credit
    ❒ Leadership Certificate
    ❒ Advanced Leadership Certificate
    ❒ State/Regional Credit

Date _____   Grade _____

Applicant Signature:_____

Foundations - The Bible
Self-Administered Exam

Name _____

Address _____

_____

INSTRUCTIONS: From your reading, complete the following questions, giving the best answer to each question. There are three types of questions: Multiple Choice, Matching , and True/False. Circle the letter of each multiple choice question which best answers or completes the statement. Indicate whether the statement is true by writing the letter "T," or false by writing the letter "F" in the blank provided for the True/False questions. Write the letter which best corresponds to the statement or term in the blank provided for the matching questions.

Unit One

1. All of the following are reasons to understand the importance of studying the Bible, except:
   a. It is a book through which God communicates to us.
   b. It helps us to be knowledgeable of the world's situations.
   c. It shows us how to be cleansed from sin.
   d. It fosters victorious and fruitful Christian living.
   e. It discovers sin and convicts us of it.

2. Revelation refers to:
   a. The necessity of uncovering the hidden mysteries of God's nature.
   b. The reception and recording of truth.
   c. The communication of truth to fallen man.
   d. The imparting of truth, by God to man, which could not be otherwise known
   e. The means by which truth is seen and understood.

3. Inspiration refers to:
   a. The necessity of uncovering the hidden mysteries of God's nature.
   b. The means by which truth is seen and understood.
   c. The communication of truth to fallen man.
   d. The imparting of truth, by God to man, which could not be otherwise known
   e. The reception and recording of truth.

4. T   F   The books of the Bible (27 in the Old Testament and 39 in the New Testament) were written over a period of 2500 years by about 36 different authors.

Match the following nine literary divisions with the corresponding books:

5. _____ The Books of the Law   A. Matthew
6. _____ The Historical Books   B. Isaiah
7. _____ The Major Prophets   C. Leviticus
8. _____ The Poetic Books   D. Philippians
9. _____ Biographical   E. Revelations
10. _____ The Minor Prophets   F. Joshua
11. _____ Pauline Epistles   G. James
12. _____ General Epistles   H. Job
13. _____ Prophetical   I. Malachi

Unit Two

14. The Old Testament was mostly originally written in which of the following languages:
   a. Aramaic
   b. Hebrew
   c. Greek

15. The New Testament was mostly originally written in which of the following languages:
   a. Aramaic
   b. Hebrew
   c. Greek
   d. English
   e. French

16. Which of the following is not a division of the Hebrew Old Testament?
    a. Torah
    b. Messiah
    c. Nebhiim
    d. Kethubhim

17. The Greek translation of the Old Testament, completed in Alexandria about 285 B.C., is known as the:
    a. Vulgate
    b. Septuagint
    c. King James Version

18. The Latin translation of the Bible, completed by Jerome about 400 A.D., is known as the:
    a. Vulgate
    b. Septuagint
    c. King James Version

19. The English translation of the Bible, completed in 1611 A.D. by forty-seven scholars, is known as the:
    a. Vulgate
    b. Septuagint
    c. King James Version

20. T F   The ancient Hebrew form of the Old Testament was arranged differently than the present English Old Testament of thirty-nine books. In the process of time, a threefold classification of the Hebrew Scriptures was developed (Luke 24:44).

21. Which of the following is a proof of the authority of the Bible:
    a. The Bible claims to be the inerrant record of the revelation of God.
    b. Jesus affirmed the inerrancy and authority of the Bible.
    c. The unsurpassed unity and harmony of the Bible is proof of its divine origin.
    d. All of the above.
    e. None of the above.

22. T F Canonization concerns the recognition and collection of God-breathed, authoritative writings into the body of Holy Scriptures.

23. The Greek word *Kanon* refers to:
   a. A means of determining the value of a book by its authorship.
   b. The uncovering of truth from God to man.
   c. A reed which can be used metaphorically to refer to a standard.

24. During which century were all of the books of the New Testament universally accepted by all of the churches and their leaders:
   a. First
   b. Second
   c. Third
   d. Fourth
   e. Fifth

25. The criteria for recognizing the canonicity of a book included all of the following except:
   a. Claims
   b. Authority
   c. Living spiritual character
   d. Universality
   e. Authenticity

Match the following three individuals with his contribution to the history of the English Bible:

26. _____ John Wycliffe   a. The first to produce a portion of a printed version from the original Hebrew and Greek into English.

27. _____ William Tyndale   b. The first to produce an English translation of the Bible.

28. _____ King James I   c. Produced a major translation that was to be used both in the churches and homes.

Unit Three

29. The _____ were an Indo-European speaking people who conquered the Babylonians in the sixth century B.C.
    a. Egyptians
    b. Canaanites
    c. Assyrians
    d. Babylonians
    e. Persians

30. The _____ were the sedentary inhabitants of Palestine and southern Syria.
    a. Egyptians
    b. Canaanites
    c. Assyrians
    d. Babylonians
    e. Persians

31. The _____ were a highly developed civilization among whom Joseph and his family settled.
    a. Egyptians
    b. Canaanites
    c. Assyrians
    d. Babylonians
    e. Persians

32. The _____ were the heirs to the Sumerians and Akkadians in southern Mesopotamia.
    a. Egyptians
    b. Canaanites
    c. Assyrians
    d. Babylonians
    e. Persians

33. _____ was a powerful state that exercised control as far west as the Mediterranean Sea.
    a. Egypt
    b. Canaan
    c. Assyria
    d. Babylonia
    e. Persia

34. The _____ were a righteous sect that liked the attention and praises of men and did much to polish the outward appearance. They represented the prevailing religious beliefs of the majority of the Jewish people.
   a. Pharisees
   b. Saducees
   c. Essenes
   d. Herodians

35. The _____ were a sect of high priests, wealthy, influential and aristocratic families, most of whom were ready to embrace Hellenic culture. Many of them were members of the Sanhedrin.
   a. Pharisees
   b. Saducees
   c. Essenes
   d. Herodians

Match the following eight people with their significance:

36. _____ Alexander the Great

37. _____ Ptolemy

38. _____ Antiochus Epiphanes

39. _____ Judas Maccabeus

40. _____ Pompey

41. _____ Mattathias

42. _____ Herod the Great

a. A Roman General

b. Initially led the Jews in rebellion against the Syrians.

c. The greatest military genius in the ancient world.

d. Helped develop the great city of Alexandria in Egypt.

e. King of Palestine when Christ was born.

f. Credited with saving Judaism from paganism.

g. Launched a systematic program for the extermination of Judaism.

Unit Four

Match the following descriptions with the appropriate person:

43. _____ Abraham   a. A judge who was called by God to be a prophet

44. _____ Isaac   b. Prophet of the Babylonian Captivity who draws a compar son between the temporary earthly kingdoms and the eternal kingdom of Christ

45. _____ Jacob   c. The 'weeping prophet' who laments the sin of Judah and its destruction.

46. _____ Joseph   d. One of the greatest of men in the Bible to whom was the first great promise given and through whom all the people of the earth were blessed.

47. _____ Moses   e. The king of Israel who was the builder of the great temple in Jerusalem.

48. _____ Joshua   f. Known as the "prophet of righteousness," his writing is known as the work of a literary genius.

49. _____ Samuel   g. The "Son of 'Promise'" who was the father of twins.

50. _____ Saul   h. He was used by God to deliver Israel out of Egypt.

51. _____ David   i. He led the Jews in the rebuilding of the walls around Jerusalem.

52. _____ Solomon   j. A prophet who used object lessons to get his point across.

53. _____ Isaiah   k. He was made a ruler in Egypt so his family could be saved.

54. _____ Jeremiah   l. He led Israel in the conquest of Canaan.

55. _____ Ezekiel   m. The king who was not allowed to build the Temple because he was a man of war.

56. ____ Nehemiah   n. The first king of Israel who was rejected by God.

57. ____ Daniel   o. The patriarch who was became a "prince with God."

Match the following events with the description of their significance:

58. ____ The call of Abraham   a. "Every man did that which was right in his own eyes."

59. ____ The Exodus   b. The rebuilding of the temple and Jerusalem.

60. ____ The covenant at Sinai   c. The Passover was established.

61. ____ The Levitical sacrifices   d. His family was entrusted with the knowledge of God, His laws, His will, and His plan of salvation.

62. ____ The rule of the Judges   e. The government turned from a theocracy to a monarchy.

63. ____ The Monarchy   f. The giving of the Decalogue.

64. ____ The divided kingdom   g. Given to demonstrate the need of salvation and foreshadowed the grace dispensation.

65. ____ The exile in Babylon   h. During it, what we know as Judaism arose.

66. ____ The return from captivity   i. A time of disobedience brings the inevitable results of God's judgments.

Unit Five

67. T   F   Philippians is one of the General Epistles.

68. Which of the following Gospels focuses on the gospel Christ, the Son of Man.
   a. The Gospel of Matthew
   b. The Gospel of Mark
   c. The Gospel of Luke
   d. The Gospel of John

69. The return of Christ and the establishment of His Kingdom is the focus of which of the following:
    a. Romans
    b. Ephesians
    c. 1 Thessalonians
    d. Titus
    e. Revelation

70. T   F   John the Baptist began his ministry some two years before Jesus began His public ministry.

71. John the Baptist preached which of the following types of baptism:
    a. A baptism for the remission of sins.
    b. A baptism which showed the answer of a good conscience toward God.
    c. A baptism of repentance.
    d. A baptism which regenerated the one being baptized.

72. T   F   The gospel writers were concerned to give a complete record of the events of Jesus' life.

73. To which of the temptations did Jesus respond, "...Thou shalt worship the Lord thy God, and Him only shalt thou serve."
    a. Turning the stone into bread.
    b. Leaping off the pinnacle.
    c. Worshiping Satan.

74. T   F   When Jesus ministered to the Samaritan woman it was the first indication that Jesus was to come only to the Jews.

75. The Beatitudes are included in which of Jesus sermons:
    a. The Olivet Discourse.
    b. The Sermon on the Mount.
    c. The Bread of Life Discourse.
    d. The Good Shepherd Sermon.

76. T   F   On the rock of Peter's revelation of the divinity of Jesus, Christ said He would build His church.

77. T F After Paul's conversion he was at first mistrusted by many of the Christians because of his persecution of the church.

78. All of the following are true of Paul, except:
  a. He was born in Rome.
  b. He studied at the feet of Gamaliel.
  c. He knew at least the Hebrew and Greek languages.
  d. Before his conversion he was a Pharisee.
  e. He learned the skill of tent making as a young boy

Match the following six events to either the:
  First Missionary Journey = a
  Second Missionary Journey = b
  Third Missionary Journey = c
  Trip to Rome = d

79. _____ Paul was shipwrecked on the island of Malta.
80. _____ Three-year ministry at Ephesus.
81. _____ Established the church on Cyprus.
82. _____ Preached to the elders from Ephesus.
83. _____ Was jailed in Philippi.
84. _____ Was accompanied by Barnabas and John Mark.

85. T F The proposal which was agreed to at the council at Jerusalem maintained the necessity of circumcision for the Gentiles.

86. All of the following are true about Peter, except:
  a. At Jerusalem he championed the cause of the Gentiles.
  b. He was very prominent among the twelve disciples.
  c. He was present when the Holy Ghost fell at Pentecost.
  d. He wrote three of the General Epistles.
  e. It is believed he visited Rome during the later years of his ministry and was martyred about the same time as Paul.

87. Which description of the Apostle John is not true:
  a. He was the beloved disciple.
  b. He was appointed to take care of Jesus mother.
  c. He spent much of his later ministry in Ephesus.
  d. He died on the isle of Patmos.

88. T   F   The author of the epistle of James appears to have been the brother of Jesus.

89. T   F   In the genealogies of the Gospels, Luke and Matthew both record the genealogy of Joseph.

Match the following New Testament books with the appropriate description:

90. _____ Epistles to the Corinthians

a. Written to Christians wavering between Christianity and Judaism.

91. _____ Galatians

b. Written from Ephesus and Philippi to address various problems being faced in the church.

92. _____ Epistles to the Thessalonians

c. Its central theme is the liberty of the Christian religion in its emphasis on grace and faith, rather than works of the law.

93. _____ Romans

d. Centered around Paul's teaching concerning the second coming of Jesus.

94. _____ Colossians

e. The dominant theme is joy.

95. _____ Philemon

f. Written to help in the difficult work of regulating the churches on Crete.

96. _____ Ephesians

g. The theme of the book is the union of God's holy church to Christ as its Head.

97. _____ Philippians

h. Written to the person who was serving as the overseer in Ephesus.

98. _____ Epistles to Timothy

i. The theme of the book is that Christ is all-sufficient as the Lord of the universe and the Head of the Church.

99. _____ Titus

j. Written to address a personal matter.

100. _____ Hebrews

k. Written to deal with the problem of people teaching that circumcision was necessary to salvation.